T0369487

ROY HARRIS OF CUT AND SHOOT:

TEXAS BACKWOODS BATTLER

by
Roy Harris, Attorney-at-Law
and
Robin Montgomery, PhD

iUniverse, Inc.
Bloomington

Roy Harris of Cut and Shoot
Texas Backwoods Battler

iUniverse books may be ordered through booksellers or by contacting:

iUniverse
1663 Liberty Drive
Bloomington, IN 47403
www.iuniverse.com
1-800-Authors (1-800-288-4677)

ISBN: 978-1-4759-6066-2 (sc)
ISBN: 978-1-4759-6068-6 (e)
ISBN: 978-1-4759-6067-9 (dj)

Library of Congress Control Number: 2012921154

Printed in the United States of America

iUniverse rev. date: 11/13/2012

CONTENTS

CONTENTS

Dedication and Acknowledgments

This is book is dedicated to the memory of J.T. Montgomery, early mentor and coach of Roy Harris and father and inspiration of Robin Montgomery.

Special thanks also to Fran Swann for working with Roy to record his memories and to Wynne Harris, Frances Lane and Joy Renee Montgomery for services in editing.

About the Co-Author

(Since the book is about one of the co-authors, Roy Harris, mentioned here is the other co-author, Robin Montgomery):

Robin Navarro Montgomery is a native of Conroe, Texas and holds a PhD from the University of Oklahoma. His professional background includes a career as university professor at Southwestern Oklahoma State University and Oxford Graduate School, along with four years as professor of international relations for a graduate program in Europe for US military officers. Among his organizational experiences, he is a member of the international Oxford Society of Scholars. He has published extensively in both political science and local history, articles, books and newspaper columns. His previous books on local history include: *The History of Montgomery County, Texas*; *Cut'n*

Shoot, Texas; Tortured Destiny: Lament of a Shaman Princess(historical novel); *Historic Montgomery County: An Illustrated History; Indians and Pioneers of Original Montgomery County; March to Destiny: Cultural Legacy of Stephen F. Austin's Original Colony* and with Joy Montgomery, *Navasota*(Arcadia images of America Series).

FOREWORD:

Generations of fighting Harris blood exploded through Roy Harris's veins that night in 1958 as he stood in the boxing ring in Los Angeles in the midst of thousands. A rare item among the world's top heavyweights, an honor student with a college degree and with an officer's commission in the U.S. Army, tonight he was facing the undefeated world heavyweight champion.

Floyd Patterson had obtained the heavyweight crown at an earlier age than any other man in history at the time. As champion, he seldom, if ever, had even been knocked down. How could a rustic backwoodsman turned gentleman-scholar-soldier cope with such a challenge? What strange events had conspired to create the meeting of such a contrast in pugilistic antagonists?

This book is, in part, the story of how and why Roy Harris emerged from backwoods obscurity to the pinnacle of fistic heaven, a heavyweight title bout. It further records key aspects of Roy's life after boxing and how his earlier upbringing impacted on a success few fighters of his statue have enjoyed. But the book is fundamentally the record of the rapidly vanishing breed, which spawned and nourished Roy—the rugged individualistic frontiersmen of the oil-rich Texas thicket country. It is about those individuals who knew who they were and what they wanted out of life and who were not afraid to fight for their beliefs, even against the interloping "boomers" when the oil towns were new. In short, this is the story of the stuff which has made American great, and which that country is searching desperately to recapture.

INTRODUCTION:

CUT AND SHOOT'S A STATE OF MIND

This book is in part, a revision of a book which I, Robin Montgomery, published in 1984*. This time, however, recollections straight from Roy Harris, himself, as of the years 2011-2012, are interjected at pivotal points. This adds Roy's perspective with hindsight to tales told to me as a youth by various principal characters in the saga of Cut and Shoot. The words of the later Roy Harris are italicized. Also new is the use of the term "Cut and Shoot," the now official name of the town, instead of "Cut'n Shoot" as in my previous book.

In these pages, tales are told of the Harris clan's travels from far off lands and of their adventures in the San Jacinto River watershed in Southeast Texas. Also told is the story of Roy Harris's rise from the backwoods of Cut and Shoot to international fame.

Roy's father, Henry Harris Sr., was the closest friend of my father, J.T. Montgomery, who was for forty years an administrator in the Conroe, Texas School System. On many occasions, I sat with my dad, Henry and others, around the clan's campfires in the dark of the moon listening with rapture to stories that would captivate the impressionable mind of one so young. My father recorded many of those conversations and from these tapes came much of the dialect used to authenticate the conversations.

I grew up with "Little Henry" Harris, the third son of "Big" Henry, who was in my grade at school. Both of us grew up behind Tobe and Roy Harris who were a little older. Young Henry and my hero in the early years was the handsome and multitalented Campbell "Wildman" Woodman of Cut and Shoot, who was, in turn, a few years older than Tobe and Roy. Wildman could play most any instrument, he could sing, his mind was quick and he had a quicker left hook and the hardest right cross of any amateur of his day in the state of Texas. He later, like Roy for a short while, became a popular schoolteacher in the Conroe School System.

One of my most vivid memories of Cut and Shoot is of a time in the late summer of 1948, just before my tenth birthday, when poison ivy ravaged my entire body, head and all. My parents had carried me to the local doctors in Conroe to no avail, and then specialists in Houston were consulted. I remember that hot August day when I walked feverishly through the wildwood of Cut and Shoot with "Big" Henry and Wildman.

When they reached the saltwater pit a few hundred yards from the Harris home, Henry lifted me bodily and threw him in. Saltwater pits are used to store the brine from the inner earth in oil field operations in order to keep the salt from contaminating the adjacent ground. The inner chambers of Hades, reserved for the Devil, himself, are cool and pleasant compared to that briny pit. Every nerve in my body ushered electrical currents to that part of my brain that governed exploding pain. In the awful depths of that poisoned hollow in the ground I wished upon King Henry and his Cut and Shoot court the fate of the Biblical City of Gomorrah which had suffered destruction from fire and brimstone ages earlier.

I surfaced and Henry pulled me from the tortured waters with the greeting, "Welcome to Cut and Shoot!" I never complained about the dreadful experience because my father warned me not to. Even though I continued to follow the clans through the toxic plants of the greenwood and to sit around the campfires, I never again experienced a serious case of poison ivy or poison oak. I scaled as clean as did Naaman after following the orders of the Biblical Elisha to dip himself in the River Jordan to cure his leprosy. Henry told me that that was the way he cured the mange of his hunting dogs and that a few years earlier Wildman had undergone the same treatment. I asked Wildman what he thought when Henry threw him in. The poetic Wildman answered, "It turned my toes and burnt my bones, but I knew I'd be free of poison oak, from then on."

With the memory of the bath in that salty caldron gripping my mind, I sat down to write the first edition of this book, recording just a few of the deeds of the noble gentry of the greenwoods of Cut and Shoot whom I have ever revered. I tried to show how they had lived rough and happy, course and clean, under laws inherited from their Scotch-Irish ancestors who ran the Appalachian ridges before they adopted the Ozarks and Indian Territory. Earlier ancestors had fought against English Kings for the values of freedom, self-determination and respect. The Cut and Shoot clans lived by those values and under the Constitution of the United States, which Henry Harris said was "laid down for all creation to live by."

Until the early 1930s, the Cut and Shoot clansmen enjoyed what to them was an ideal existence, hunting, fishing and passing on stories of their ancestors. Though there were occasional clashes between the clans, nothing ever flared into open warfare. The means of livelihood of the inhabitants of that vast and tangled land were varied; farming, raising livestock and sometimes working in the oil fields were among their occupational pursuits. Supplementing these endeavors, one thing was common to most, hog-raising. The range was free and the men were as wild and free as the savage "tush hogs" they herded.

I grew up on a sandy loam farm and during most of my younger days; the area we lived in was under the Open Range law for livestock. This meant that farm animals did not have to be fenced. They could roam on the open range. Farmers with crops were responsible for fencing their own fields with stock proof fencing to keep the animals out. We were farmers and raised farm animals. We never had much money, but we always had plenty of good food to eat. The chief means of our livelihood was from hog- raising, farming, livestock and my father's job as an oil-field worker.

We always had several hundred head of hogs running wild in the woods, which we depended on for food. We did not feed them; they ate acorns, roots, grub worms and whatever else they could find. There was really not enough for the hogs to eat, and they had a hard time surviving; often times in late summer, they would get cholera and would die. When the faulty acorns started falling in September, they would begin putting on weight. During October and November, the hogs would get very fat due to eating so many acorns. We actually began killing and processing the hogs when the first norther (cold spell) arrived. We put pork up many ways for later use.

We had to be creative in the way we preserved the meat, as we did not have a freezer or refrigerator as we had no electricity.(In fact, we did not get electricity until I was around 17 years of age when REA brought electricity to our neighborhood.) Other methods had to be used for preserving the meat. We smoked some, put up some in jars and cans, ground up some for sausage, but most was salted away. A layer of shorts (grinding off of grains of wheat) would be put down in a barrel, with a layer of salted pork with another layer of shorts, continuing with the layering until the container was full. When complete, the pork would be completely covered by the shorts and salt. The salt would pull the moisture from the meat, and the shorts would absorb the moisture. This would preserve the pork until we used it at a later time.

The salt could be washed off and the pork could be cooked any way it was needed. It could be breaded and fried as pork chops or boiled with a pot of rice for soup. It was still delicious.

All of the parts of the hog were used. The fat was rendered to make grease. The hide was fried or baked which made the grease and cracklings. Cracklings were eaten as a treat or used to make bread. The intestines were cleaned and stuffed with ground *pork and seasonings to make the link sausage. The hams, along with the stuffed sausage, were hung in a smokehouse where a fire of hickory wood was kept smoking; the meat absorbed the smoke and the heat which cured it. A lot of the liquid was removed from the ground sausage and hams to help preserve them. They could be kept hanging indefinitely until they were eaten. Pork was plentiful and one of the main sources of food for our family, as well as for the predators.*

While hog raising among the Cut and Shoot clansmen was significant, theirs was a lifestyle characterized by self-sufficiency in multiple areas such as cattle raising, farming, hunting and fishing.

We raised our crops for our family's food and for food for our animals. I can't remember our selling produce. We had ducks, geese, turkeys, cattle, goats, hogs and chickens as well as fighting game chickens. We ate a lot of chickens as well as the eggs they produced. My uncle Bob would eat only the game chickens and not the tame ones saying that the game ones were "good eating". All ran wild in the woods around the house. We had a pond where the ducks and geese swam and hunted for bugs and crawfish. We fed them corn and maize, but they still had a hard time surviving the predators, like possums, raccoons, foxes and chicken hawks and owls. Uncle Bob used to say that if he had a hen that could not whip a chicken hawk, he did not want her around his place. He said,

"If the chicken hawk came down after a baby chick, he would leave with a lot less feathers than he had when he landed." The mama hen would stay after him until he flew off and left her babies alone. We also caught fish from the pond and from a larger lake across the field.

There were no definite plans for the chickens and only a few specific nests for them to lay their eggs. We nailed five gallon cans on the side of the trees about 5 feet from the ground with grass in them for nests for the chickens. Some chose to use them and others found more interesting places to nest. My sister, Frances, tells of finding eggs in our house where the chickens had gone in and laid them.

We had no screens, and the windows were usually open in our home to catch the breeze, and though we tried to keep them out of the house, the chickens often managed to sneak in and find a place to lay their eggs. Frances said that many times she found the eggs either on her bed or on the dresser. I also found them on my dresser in my room one time. One thing about their laying in the house, the eggs were easier to find than looking out in the woods for them. Chicken houses were built later for them to roost and lay eggs, but most of the chickens liked to roost in the trees and lay their eggs in the woods or in the cans on the trees or in our house.

With Roy Harris, I have tried to show in this book, in an authentic way, how the self-sufficient and relatively peaceful existence of the clans received a severe challenge on the eve of Roy's birth due to events surrounding the great oil strikes of 1931 and 1932. The harvesting of black gold in their land made it necessary for the clans to unite under Henry and his brothers, Jack and Bob Harris, to defend their property and possessions from the interloping oil field "boomers." These dramatic times spawned the colorful careers of Tobe and Roy Harris and set the stage for the Cut and Shoot of today. That once primitive and savage land has become a cosmopolitan suburb of Houston and the home to several world famous personalities, including, in addition to Roy, Debra Maffett, Miss America of 1983, and Larry Butler, of grand ole opry fame.

More than just the name of a place, the words Cut and Shoot have come to signify an attitude venerating the values of freedom, self-determination, self-respect and reverence for God Almighty, values nourished and bequeathed to the world by the noble woodsmen along the banks of the San Jacinto River in southeast Texas.

Truly, Cut and Shoot's a state of mind.

Cut'n Shoot Texas: Roy Harris—Battler from the Backwoods (Austin: Eakin Press, 1984).

Chapter I

BAPTISM IN BOXING

There is an ocean of trees interlaced with vines in southeast Texas, from which the morning dew drips upon a spongy, swampy ground. A sort of stickiness exudes from the humor in the rotting wilderness and mingles with overhanging ooze, which boils in sooty clouds out of the Gulf of Mexico. So dense is the foliage and so tangled are the semi-tropical thickets that wolves still prowl from its fringes into the subdivisions of such metropolitan centers as Houston, Beaumont and Conroe. Two forks in the upper reaches of the San Jacinto River cup a portion of the forest. The bottom half of the cup contains the environs of Cut and Shoot.

When Roy was young, the wilderness of Cut and Shoot was still as savage as it was when it turned back the explorations of the Spanish Dons two hundred years before. Upon leaving the Ozarks around the turn of the century, Roy's grandfather, John Wesley Harris, established permanent roots in Montgomery County where many of his children, grandchildren and great grandchildren grew up in a stable environment. The territory had an open range for livestock. Owners would roundup, mark or brand the offspring each year. There were so few settlers in the broad expanse that it was difficult to determine ownership of the wild razorback shoats rooting between the East and West San Jacinto Rivers. This led on occasion to clashes between the clans. In such an environment, pugilistic skill was a must.

When you think of a ring, you think of something round; in boxing, the ring is square. The ring we used was made of three ropes tied to four different posts to make the corners of the ring. The ropes were very loose but helped to keep the boxer inside. The ropes were wrapped with burlap to prevent rope burns if a boxer went into the ropes. Before the ring was built, the ring we had been using had barbed wire on two sides of it instead of rope. We soon learned to "stay off the ropes" because the barbed wire was much more dangerous and hurt us more than someone's fist.

Our first set of gloves came from some of our neighbors who received a set of four gloves for Christmas; they had used the gloves to box one another not knowing how to box or what to do and decided that they did not like them.

While boxing during those early years growing up, we knew nothing about mouthpieces and cups, headgear or hand wraps. I fought bare footed in cut off blue jeans and thought I looked great! However, as I began to fight in boxing tournaments in other towns, I learned to use all the protective gear I could to protect myself. I really did not like to get hit.

My brother, Tobe, wanted those gloves because he liked to fight and wanted to box somebody every day. I was the handiest sparring partner, but we had no gloves. Tobe made a deal to trade four ducks for the set of four gloves. We had to catch the ducks and take them to the boys who had the gloves to make the trade. That set of gloves got boxing started in Cut and Shoot and was the beginning of my career. Tobe was twelve years of age, and I was ten.

In order to cope with the irrepressible Tobe, Roy was forced to develop a Spartan routine.

I worked out every day, seven days a week, even when I did not want to. We may have missed a few days, and I did not like getting my nose blooded all the time. One time I was trying to avoid having to box Tobe, although my father and my uncle wanted us to work out. Anyway, they lured me down a trail into the woods about 100 yards from the house. There my father and uncle put the gloves on me.

Taking advantage of an opportunity, I managed to escape and ran toward the house, hollering for Mama; I knew she would protect me and keep them from making me fight. As I ran toward the house, I could see Tobe was catching up with me, so I turned around and stuck my left jab in his face. Tobe went down, and I ran and made it to Mama. As I knew she would, Mama saved me from fighting that day.

As time went by I began to get heavier than Tobe. Now when we fought, I did not get a bloody nose all the time. I finally was able to out box Tobe. Other boys began to show up in the evening and box with us so that we had others to box with besides each other. In our earlier days, there were some older boys that were bigger who boxed with us and took it easy on us until we began to get big enough and learn enough to outbox them; we would then have to take it easy on them.

Many boys learned to box at our home because of my dad helping them. Some became leaders in the community as they grew up because of their boxing and having Henry work with them. He believed in working on self-confidence as well as on boxing skills. I think he could get more out of a boy than anyone I have ever seen. He encouraged them to do their best in whatever they attempted. This included me and my brothers and sisters. It seems that all of us wanted to do our best at all times to please him. We did not want to let him down in his expectations of us.

Backwoods wisdom was a key factor in Roy Harris's rise to the heights of boxing's elite. A prime example comes from conditions surrounding Roy's first ring encounter against a bona fide "blue chip" opponent. It was in the Conroe boxing tournament in 1949:

Waiting for his fight, Roy rested his hundred and nineteen pounds of bantamweight muscle in a wicker chair on the stage of Conroe's High School gymnasium. The fifteen-year-old Roy was restless, yet calm. Wildman Woodman was lying on an army cot giving advice to his neighbor, Roy, who was calm as well.

"Just fight the Killer like you'd fight Tobe," Wildman advised. "Don't take 'nary a chance a 'tall, 'cause if you do, 'taint a thing me and Henry and Tobe can do to help you." The main thing is to keep your chin behind your shoulder so's his right hand won't hurt you none. The fight will last longer if you do that, and don't dance."

Wildman, the recently crowned light heavyweight champion of Texas, was to fight the main event tonight. He was almost asleep in spite of the hubbub of the crowd out there in the gymnasium. Roy leaned from the wicker chair to get his final words of counsel.

"Your left fore arm gotta be high up a'counterin'. He throws his powder from way back close to the ring ropes, so ride it from the outside and counter. Now warm up, and wake me up when you go on."

Roy knew little about warming up, but he did his best. Some of the other fighters behind the drawn curtain on the stage watched him do his jogging calisthenics, and then looked at each other in mingled amazement and indeed, amusement. Each were champions in various weights of their respective Golden Gloves regionals and some, like the sleeping Wildman, had the word Texas printed in gold on their black boxing trunks to prove they had represented the Lone Star State in the Tournament of Champions in Chicago.

None of the young men commented on what he saw. Each felt a mismatch was about to be offered up to the gods of greed and glory. Certainly, they felt sorry for the awkward appearing lad. Who wouldn't? Wasn't he breaking sweat to climb into the ring with one of the best bantamweights in the nation, a fighter who was multiple years his senior?

A scrawny country kid against a grown man skilled in the arts and crafts of the trade! Along the rugged amateur trail they had seen many mistakes made in matching, but nothing to compare with this one. Oh well, it couldn't last longer than a couple of flurries, they assumed. Then the youngster would be out of his misery. At least he wouldn't be cut to pieces.

Harry "Killer" Tawana danced out on the stage sending his fists through the empty air in graceful quest for an imaginary target. He bounded lightly along on the balls of his feet, bending his knees in oily rhythm to a rolling motion of his shoulders. As he worked, something akin to hate seemed to seep into his eyes, causing the lids to swell, although grim determination might have influenced the swelling. The rest of his face was set in pale drawn lines that bespoke his undaunted will to win.

Roy continued to lumber through his exercises, paying little attention to his panther-like opponent. A clang of the gong muffling through the curtains signaled finis to the bout that had been in progress. It also served as a signal for Roy and the Killer to put on their robes and make ready.

Roy shook the army cot to awaken Wildman, and then he sauntered down a flight of dark steps to a doorway that opened into the gymnasium. There he waited. He wanted the champ to enter the ring and finish most of his showing off without being in there with him to witness the spectacle. Also he wanted Wildman to have time to get the sleep out of his system and join him.

The spectators had for several years watched the best talent in Texas and Louisiana battle in the Conroe Tournament. Tawana was good. They knew that. Their only question was who, in those two states, was foolish enough to let him maul him into a corner.

Tobe had fought earlier in the evening against a regional champion and downed him. That was gratifying because the Cut and Shoot scrapper was by the far the underdog. Each bout brought on new surprises. Now Tawana was up there to entertain them. All of this was just an exciting prelude to the main event, which would pit John Tennis of Sam Houston State College against the pride of the big thicket, Wildman Woodman.

As Roy walked down the aisle to his corner, a touch of sadness daunted the half-smile that dangled around the dimples of his cheeks. That grim echo of sadness served to surround him with an aura of mystery.

Silence seized the crowd as the rank backwoodsman climbed through the ropes. Everybody knew him. He was one of the Cut and Shoot Harris's: the son of Henry, the nephew of Jack and Bob, the brother of Tobe. They knew him, so they reasoned he was too unseasoned to fight the awesome Tawana. As an occasional gasp pierced the silence, the bell sounded to start the fight.

As Tawana saw a left jab pecking toward him he moved his head downward and to the right in order to counter with his left hand to the stomach. He had worked this simple maneuver a hundred times. This time the jab failed to spend itself but curved into a wicked hook to his temple. But for the sliding motion of Tawana's head, a motion known in boxing circles as rolling with the punch, the Killer's face would have been wreathing in pain.

Roy backed to the ropes and waited. While he waited, he studied. While he studied, the facsimile of a tempestuous typhoon gone mad swarmed upon him. Lefts and rights, uppercuts, followed by crosses . . . jabs, jabs, and jabs. Then the stars appeared to Roy as though the eye of the typhoon had calmed him.

A sense of sinking knocked on the door of Roy's brain, but before the brain could answer a jagged thunderbolt tore out of the whirlwind before him and landed with a ringing, stunning impact on his cheekbone. The second ring rope became a fulcrum to sustain his rigid body, which was seesawing half in and half out of the place of battle.

Tobe caught hold of his brother's shoulders and pushed him back into the ring. As the lad landed on his knees, Bill Hopson, the referee, began to count towards ten. By the count of seven the brave and determined lad from Cut and Shoot was up and back into the fray. Soon the fighter's arms were locked along the ring ropes, causing Hobson to call for a break, separating them.

Sparks of excitement filled the gymnasium, driving the spectators to the edge of their seats. Tawana had taken two right hands to the head just after the break. That was much too much for the monarch of the bantamweights, especially after he had been humiliated along the ring ropes. Grief like a capital G seemed to appear on his gloves, and the message traveled with a bang to Roy's body. A left, a right, two lefts landed on target.

Then Roy countered with a right which straightened at the elbow with the shoulder and with enough kick behind it to snap Tawana's head back. Two left hooks and another straight right caused his head to resemble a kite caught in the windy cross currents of the spring equinox.

Roy swatted his adversary across the ring, digging deep into his lithe body with his right. Roy's left hand played tic-tac-toe on the right side of Tawana's head. So intent was he on the combinations that he forgot that repeated digs to the body with a right could invite disaster from an experienced gladiator such as Tawana, who knew how to jab a left straight and hard to the button. And so the blow came, but fortunately just before the bell, allowing the staggering Roy time to recover in his corner.

By his side in that corner, Henry Harris reflected, as usual, supreme confidence in his offspring. "Drop the hammer on him, son," was all that he admonished.

Wildman was not sleepy anymore, but he was still feeling lazy. The only antidote to his lethargy would be to grease and glove him up and send him into the ring. Now he said nothing to Roy as he took the rubber mouthpiece to a nearby water bucket, dropped it in to soak and sat down next to his sweetheart. Wildman wanted Roy to win, but he also wanted to win his fair lady. He knew Roy was doing all right and would fight like he wanted to anyhow.

Hobson came over to the corner to check on Roy, to make sure he was able to continue. Upon expressing the courtesy of a quick "yes sir" to the question, Roy directed his attention diagonally across the ring to his opponent in the opposite corner. Their studied gazes seemed to meet in the center of the ring and to clash in invisible mayhem. Each pondered the other as he formulated destruction.

As Roy was thus engaged, Tobe dropped to his knees in the corner to give sage pugilistic counsel to his brother.

And so the fighters resumed their places in the center of the ring. Tawana threw a left that missed. He followed with a sizzling right that did the same thing. They tied up in Roy's corner, where the referee separated them. Roy then quickly swung an uppercut that grazed Tawana's chin, while retreating along the ropes to a neutral corner.

Tawana followed through, attracted by a hidden magnet placed somewhere on the person of his opponent from Cut and Shoot. In response, Roy's right hand winged high before it dipped and snapped across the Killer's left forearm on its way to where the jawbone is hinged to the left side of the head.

The impact shook Tawana. He hesitated while his numbed nerves staggered to the brain for fresh instructions on how to combat the riled young Texan.

Another right spun Tawana. A shrieking left hook bruised the tissue connecting the ribs on his starboard side as he spun. Instinct, not the brain, caused him to seek to enwrap Roy in a clinch.

Before Tawana could accomplish his goal, Roy blistered his gums and lips with three trip-hammer jabs. This was no bantering, bowing bout between gentlemen under the governorship of Marquis of Queensbury rules, but rather a raw lumberjack brawl in which the law of the Yukon prevailed. This law was survival of the fittest. The Killer, himself, was swinging at anything that looked or smelled of Harris.

The referee, Bill Hopson, a former baseball catcher and a good one, knew little of the rules of boxing. Besides, he liked this thing, and decided to turn the pugilists loose. After all, the spectators were screaming their approval.

Roy used every legal maneuver he could muster to fend off his determined opponent. The two fighters continued to pound each other through the second round. When Roy finally went to his corner, his dad looked at him proudly.

"Just drop the hammer on him," he advised yet again, with his voice dripping with confidence in his son.

The third round was brutal. Roy staggered his opponent who staggered him in return. Mars and Thor and all the other gods of war must have descended and convened at ringside. The crowd could not find its voice to scream. Instead, they rode their seats in a tomb-like awe while gurgles in their throats moaned for freedom.

Roy blasted wild with lefts to keep the raving "Killer" at bay while reaching deep within his inner recesses for the powder to pound him with rights. What a glorious burst of adrenaline was his.

Then it was over, and miraculously, Roy had won. A miracle had occurred in Conroe that night, as Roy Harris had beat the odds against a more skilled, experienced and classy opponent. Beholding the unexpected scene, strong people wept as a great cry went up to rock the ceiling. Tobe felt tears for the first time since he could remember. He had tried with all the ingenuity in his sixteen-year-old brain to give Roy command of the situation. Roy had fought a giant of the ring and won.

As Wildman followed Roy's bout with another victory, Conroe could dip into the future and envision gloved gladiators marching across the spangled bridge that leads to fistic glory. Cut and Shoot, that broad wilderness to the east, was undisturbed. The scattered inhabitants of that leafy expanse who had found their way into the gymnasium that memorable night, stuck their hands into their overall pockets and laughed heartily. These were men accustomed to men and boys and beast and fowl asserting themselves in the raw. Tobe, Roy and Wildman slipped out the back door and faded into the night with their kinsmen thus avoiding the shouting crowd awaiting them in the gymnasium.

Home at last at Cut and Shoot, the boys witnessed the great round orb of the moon shed yellow light that streamed across the treetops at a low angle from the West. A soft wind sighed from the same direction to bathe the moonlit clearing in unseasonable warmth for the middle of March. Long gray moss hung from the oaks that ringed the clearing and swung to and fro in the breeze. At one moment the moss rode the wind into the darkness of the forest. Then, like a pendulum, it swung back into the clearing to sparkle in the moonlight and take on the sheen of silver.

The night was at its softest. The meadowlark whispered that it was late and obtained a second to his motion by the hoot of a carnivorous barn owl deep in the forest gloom.

In the clearing the gates of glee jarred open for the backwoods denizens of Cut and Shoot. They were at their victory celebration and the night belonged to them. Guitars twanged in time to nasal singing. Fiddles broke in, to give body to the melody that soared to the beat of a dumb-bull made of cowhide stretched over the end of a hollow log and played by slapping hands like a tom-tom.

The carousal consisted of ring games played rough where men were concerned with men, but gentle, ever so gentle, with the ladies. "Wolf over the River" was a favorite. "Strawberry Roan" was another. They danced on the hard packed ground to the tune of "Old Joe Clark", "I'm Looking for the Bully of the Town," and scores of songs, fast and slow, sad and gleeful from the album of their memories reaching back to the ridge-running days of their ancestors in Arkansas.

From the innermost recesses of the tangled square miles of Cut and Shoot, the clansmen gathered to pay homage to their warriors. But none was really awed because some bold soul excelled in daring deeds or struck a telling blow to the enemy. That was expected. Their whole rhyme and reason lay in having an excuse to explode in primitive revelry.

Roy was wounded, bruised, and battered yet he flounced to the tune of the fiddle. Wildman and Tobe were better off physically but sat serenely by the ice cream freezers, turning the cranks to the tune of the music.

Uncle Bob Harris was naked from the waist up. Battle scars stood vivid against the golden hue of his skin. His beard crawled up his temples to mingle with the mat of unruly hair flowing freely from his skull. He had crowded six feet since he was sixteen. Uncle Bob was a "rounder". Tonight he circled left to the beat of the dumb-bull. Toward morning, after a night of revelry, he would be circling on tired knees in any direction his woebegone legs would carry him. Uncle Bob was a jolly fun-loving woodsman, enjoying the revere this night with a neighbor, known in the backwoods as Armadillo.

Armadillo had been to school. He had even learned to read and write his name after repeated years of experience. There were times, however, when the school authorities in Conroe had become exasperated with his antics.

One time he closed all the doors to the school auditorium and turned a particularly playful dog loose in an assembly of several hundred children. The school band was rendering a concert on the stage as the over-friendly animal announced his presence with incessant barking, jumping and romping through the crowd. So rampant was the resultant commotion and confusion that some of the children jumped from their seats, seeking to ascertain the source of the sudden excitement. Enough of the band members were distracted to cause the bewildered bandleader to temporarily halt the concert.

The coach took charge of Armadillo after that. From that day forward he wore a referee's shirt and de-cleated football shoes to school and reported to the gymnasium for daily monitoring of his activities.

Day after day Armadillo alternately charmed and aggravated his classmates and teachers with an ingenuous array of good-natured but well-placed pranks. One day he ambushed the school band on its way to a parade downtown and threw scores of tomatoes into the air over its members. Some of them fell among the marchers, distracting the rhythm of the group.

While his escapades at school became local legends, Armadillo's most dramatic encounters occurred off campus. He was a past master of matters relating to a knife. He made his own knives from the finest metal he could find and fashioned the handles with deer bones. He created them in multi-designs for different purposes. No two were alike in any respect, except for their razor sharpness. Although he never sought trouble, trouble seemed to bounce him out of the bed in the morning and tuck him in at night.

One night Armadillo was in a bar, calmly petting a house cat that had cuddled up to him, when a stranger entered the tavern and after a few drinks became extremely unruly. Soon, he had driven most of the customers away and was bragging wildly about how awesome and tough he was.

After an extended period of braggadocio, the stranger discovered Armadillo, still sitting calmly, not paying attention to his bitter ramblings. In his warped frame of mind, the stranger stalked over to Armadillo and began to threaten him, slamming his hands upon the bar for emphasis. After several moments of this tirade, Armadillo pulled out his long knife and deftly hammered it between the outstretched fingers of the riled man.

On retrieving the knife, Armadillo grinned broadly at the stranger while waving before him the sharp blade. "Isn't it just a raving beauty to behold?" he smiled at the stranger using the best grammar he could muster. "The blade seems to have a mind of its own, and just glistens when it thinks there is a chance for real excitement."

Without another word, the stranger quickly vacated the premises, leaving Armadillo to chat amicably with the customers, who returned to do him homage.

Roy felt happy at home with his people. Everything his boyish heart could desire was present . . . his kinsmen and friends, fun in the moonlight, yet he was bothered. He strolled toward the big elm tree and leaned his back against the trunk. Strains of "Strawberry Roan" poured through the night from the rustic string band. Now and then a sleeping pig over in the hog pen would dream about an ear of corn floating in the slop bucket and grunt.

As his tired eyes stared through the foliage at the stars, Roy thought how wonderful it was to be a part of the bountiful outpourings of nature and to be so close to the freshness and fragrance. Yes, even the hog pen smelled delicious tonight.

It was like a dream he had dreamed once in which he stood on the edge of a precipice looking into the mists of eternity which lay in the valley below. There he saw his father and mother swinging in swings under tall trees. The rest of his kinsmen were either picking wild flowers or wading in a clear brook, grappling for pan fish. When he awoke he found that eternity existed all around him. The happy children, his loving mother and father, the fun-loving clansmen, and the mist of the subtropical jungle of Cut and Shoot appeared to him as in his dream.

He didn't want to fight. He wanted only to pull off his shoes and let the sparkling waters of the brook run over his bare feet. He wanted to listen to the wind and study his books. Life was a complex puzzle and the answers were there for the trying. Fighting had absolutely no place in his picture of living. Even the animals didn't fight unless they had a sufficient reason, and then the weaker might run away. Life here could be like the valley of eternity, were it not for the personal and collective conflicts.

In his reminiscences, Roy said it thusly:

Boxing was a big thing in my life and opened many doors and opportunities for me that I would never have had otherwise. But, the irony of the whole situation was that I never wanted to fight. I just did. I started out sparring and wound up as a boxer. Sometimes I think that I fought to survive.

At this point, Roy referred again to the influence of his brother, Tobe and Henry, his dad:

My older brother, Tobe, was the fighter and loved to fight. He needed a sparring partner, and I was the only one available. We fought every day, unless I was lucky enough to hide and escape. I also had the encouragement and the teachings of my dad, Henry, to help me learn the correct way to fight.

For Roy Harris, then, destiny would take its course. He would be a world-class fighter.

Chapter II

ROY ACKNOWLEDGES HIS BIRTHRIGHT:

The Legacy of John Wesley Harris

During a hog roundup three weeks after the boxing tournament, most of the male members of the Harris clan, including uncles and cousins, came upon a group of fishermen on a bluff bank overlooking the west fork of the San Jacinto, just above the point where Crystal Creek empties into it. Behind the bluff was a bay gall, a swampy slew in which sweet gum trees grew in profusion in the mud flats.

The fishermen were from Houston and had spent several days searching out the river for their present camp and fishing spot. They were in no mood to be moved by a motley group decked out in coonskin caps and leather breeches, foraging for piney-wood rooters.

The hog hunters had no intention of camping on the bluff, because it was already occupied. They were merely moving leisurely down the river when the fishermen became obstinate and outspoken. The Harris's and their friends of the wild woods never hankered for a fight. They always used diplomacy in every way they could until it fizzled. Then woe unto him or them who crossed their trail!

Henry slid from his horse and gestured to the thirty fishermen in a friendly way, but the suspicious fishermen were obstinate. Then Henry began, in a calm humorous manner, to explain the skill of Armadillo with a throwing knife. While he spoke, he spread the finders of his left hand against the trunk of an ash tree and ordered Armadillo to throw between them.

Zing! Without dismounting from his pony, Armadillo threw his knife into the space between Henry's thumb and pointing finger. Henry pulled the knife from the tree and gave it an underhanded sling so that it floated back to Armadillo. He still had his left hand against the tree trunk. Zing! The knife sped again but stuck that time just to the right of the little finger.

The fishermen went pale, and they became yet paler as Henry told them that Armadillo was the worst carver among them and was "just learning how."

There were only sixteen members of the Harris clan present and several of them were boys, but the sun had not set across the river before they found themselves in undisputed possession of the river bluff. The fishermen, making excuses about better fishing down the river, had vanished.

If the fish were there, they never bothered them, because several days later another party of hog hunters found a few of the poor strangers on a walnut ridge surrounded by a canebrake, a long way from the river. They were lost, exhausted and jabbering tales about crazy wild men with long sharp knives.

The Harris's camped near the mouth of Crystal Creek. That night one of their party named Hominy drank too much from the bunghole in a white oak keg, which he carried on a packhorse with the rest of the camp supplies. He became progressively more limber legged while tending the horses, and when he staggered up to the cowhide stretched between two willows that served as a supper table, groping and gasping, he was dangerously near the bonfire.

Everyone in the camp knew to leave him alone for it was the code of Uncle Jack that anyone was privileged to drink whenever and whatever he pleased as long as he did not drink to excess as to endanger others. Jack expected the drinker to be responsible for his actions.

Only Henry could countermand the whims of his brother Jack, but he seldom chose to do so. Rather, he chose to sit idly by, regardless of the risk involved, and watch human nature unfold in its rawness and to apply his conclusions to future situations wherein a lesson could be driven sternly home.

Henry loved his brothers, Jack and Bob, but he knew they were bold and reckless, neither prone to calculate any risks they undertook. Nevertheless, he tried never to interfere with their harmless pranks. One could call Bob and Jack jolly. Henry was a planner, but all three were valiant when the chips were down.

In his drunken state Hominy lurched toward the table, clutching its edges before he fell, stiff and rigid, looking much like a great wind-blown tree. His face was so close to the fire that grease fried from his cheeks and forehead. The woodsmen watched him as he lay there by the bonfire while his face crumpled in little brown wrinkles, and the heat stifled his breathing.

Finally, Jack rose from his seat on a large muscadine vine and roused the inebriated man. He loved Hominy who had fought alongside him in many a forest feud over the ownership of certain pigs. He did not want his friend to be burned. However, he was sincere in his purpose to lower the boom on everyone drinking to excess.

As the hunters with great chunks of roasted pork in their greasy hands watched, Hominy crawled off to a cypress log, which reached from the high ground of the camp to a small island in the bay gall. Beneath the log was a dark, murky slough filled with snapping turtles and alligator gars.

Hominy was unable to walk the log so he began to coon it. As he crawled slowly along, his hands slipped, and his knees lost their leverage. Slowly he sank to a prone position with his feet trying to inch him along. With his hands dangling on both sides of the log, he slid slowly along on his chest by irregular frog kicks from first one foot then the other. Alas, however, he fell into the slough.

Night had closed in. After the hog hunters spread their pallets on piles of palmetto flags that they had gathered in the bottoms they pulled Hominy from among the slimy-crawling things abounding in the bay gall. Because of his irresponsibility, however, they left him to sober up on the hard ground. As the camp gave vent to relaxation, the moon rose to shine here and there through the treetops in a feeble attempt to help a cherry-red wood fire dispel the darkness.

Serene peace came oozing from the gloom to calm the campers as their tired muscles began to tingle the way a guitar string vibrates as the tension is ever-so-gradually unwound from its tuning key. The time for story telling had arrived, which is that time between bedding down and the coming of sleep.

In that brief hour, each had stories to tell, but Uncle Roe Brown was champion of the art. His yarns carried them back across the years to nostalgic times they all remembered. Sometimes he chose, as he did tonight, to go back even farther than most could recall.

"It was just afore a freeze which was a comin' up at sundown on George Washington's birthday back in 1859 when Lou Vina Harris gave birth to John Wesley. He was borned in a log house on the rim of a ravine close to where it ran into Mulberry Creek in Franklin County, Arkansas. His pa was named David, and he had built a tan yard at the old Harris Spring in the foothills of the Ozarks several years afore the startin' of the Civil War."

Roe, son-in-law of John Wesley Harris, licked the blackberry wine from his lips as he enlightened the latter day members of the Harris clan of their forefather's sojourns in other days in lands beyond the boundaries of Cut and Shoot, Texas. Clan-like, they were an interested group as they reclined on the mossy thicket floor and watched the reflections of their campfire flicker among the ferns only to fade as it met the moonlight.

They were quiet and reflective because each remembered a treasured fragment of family lore that had been passed on at random in an incidental and informal way by older members of the family on other nights around other firesides. Now they listened reverently as the present patriarch of the family fastened those fragments together.

"On towards midnight after John Wesley was born it got colder than a tree full of snowbirds a fixing to swarm. The Seminole squaw who midwifed his bornin', froze out there in the blizzard afore she got home. A buck Indian found her next day near the Owl Nest Rock. He told Mr. David Harris that his son would grow up to be wise and wild and never content to live outside the woods. That Indian sign is still on Henry and Tobe and Roy and all the rest of John Wesley's children and grandchildren. Take Roy there. He might be the fightin' champion of the world someday, but he will always live down close to a creek."

Roy stirred himself and lazily shifted his weight so that he lay on his side with his head resting on the heel of his left hand. He held a stem of crowfoot grass in his mouth with the idle fingers of his other hand as he indolently gazed into the fire. His black hair blended so well with the wall of night behind him that when the mild west wind shifted a few strands across his forehead the strands looked like little shadows from out of the forest.

Roy and all of the clansmen were tall with the exception of Uncle Bob. All of them were handsome, robust men who would have excelled in the company of ordinary men.

Roy's gaze left the fire and fell on Uncle Bob. As Roy nibbled gingerly at the crowfoot grass with his front teeth and studied the face of his loyal, fun loving uncle, his thoughts hurried back into his happy childhood. When he thought of what Roe had said about the Indian sign, he wondered why he should ever want to leave the thicket. He sighed in contentment and listened as his Uncle Roe continued:

"Grandpa David farmed, fiddled, and ran a tan yard. While John Wesley was growin' up, he read often from the Bible. He even learned to read from it and to talk like it. He had a photographic memory and could quote much of the Bible word for word, and when he pronounced his judgment on you it sounded like the wrath of God. Lots of other folks heard when he got holy righteous in a temper and they shook and trembled like they had the swamp fever. He never cut his hair 'cause he read somewhere that it was unreligious. He didn't exactly believe he'd be condemned if he cut it, but he wore it long. His bright red hair glistened in the sunlight. When he got to be about middle aged, he snipped it and made a bridle for ole Ben W. out of it.

"John Wesley was freckle-faced, and when he got on ole Ben W. and sauntered down the trail with that bridle plaited out of his red hair, his Aunt Nitha used to say: 'John Wesley, you are like all the Harris's; you are redheaded now, but your hair will turn coal black before you die. Your Uncle John was the only one who died before his hair turned. But it did turn jet black while was on the cooling board."

After experiencing a gaze at the moon for a moment, Roe added, "come to think on it, even John Wesley's hair came back black after a siege with pneumonia. "

Roy looked quickly through the flames to the opposite side of the clannish circle to where his older brother Tobe lay relaxed with his head pillowed on a tow sack that contained a fifty-foot trammel net. The same west wind that puffed his own black hair blew long red ringlets across his brother's face and shoulders.

Tobe sprawled there in the thicket like a Viking transformed from an ancient Saxon shore. Olaf the Red or Eric the Red could not have been endowed with more physical perfection. Indeed they might have been the ancestors of this sleepy forest youth, for had not the Harris's journeyed to America from an England that once had succumbed to sea rovers from the lands of the Danes and Goths?

Roy knew, because he had been told many times, that his brother Tobe was the one most acculturated to the Harris characteristics and that he, himself, was more attuned, than his brother, to his mother's side of the family. That was the reason that he anticipated the next words of his Uncle Roe. He was curious and wanted to study his brother while his uncle talked.

He knew his brother's interest lay with an alligator in the nearby bay gall making a churning sound through the wilderness night, with his bellowing. Tobe had always loved alligators and had wrestled them amid the reeds and cypress knees along the margin of the marshes. Earlier in the evening Tobe had reminisced with his kinsmen, when the monster in the morass was silent, but now his thoughts had been called to the bay gall by a series of bellows.

"Now you take Tobe there," Roe was saying. "He is more like his grandpa than any one of his kids or grandkids. John Wesley was six feet two and a half in his stocking feet, and when he was young, his red hair came clear down to his belt. He walked straight as an Indian. He had Indian in him, Cherokee. He wore a long handled mustache, and his eyes were black. When his hair turned black, it curled. He was a husky old gentleman, about the strongest man I ever did see. He could take a hundred pound anvil by the horn with one hand and swing it arm's length above his head."

Roy still watched the golden glow of the firelight play in Tobe's long red hair. He had seen Tobe take hold of an anvil of the same weight and sling it above his head with both hands, but he knew that someday, with practice, his brother would stand in glory like his grandfather, shaking the heavy anvil with his strong right arm toward the heavens. He also knew that the time would soon be at hand for a trial at the anvil himself.

Courage and wisdom were taken for granted by his family. Strength had to be proven. How he longed for the strength of his brother who lay so unconcerned and uninterested with his flaming red head resting on the tow sack; Tobe's ear was attuned to the primitive complaints of the alligators floating in the dark limpid waters down there in the moonlit moor!

Roy scratched a yearling tick that was lodged between his shoulder blade and backbone, and as he flicked it into the fire, he spun his mind into a reverie of backwoods philosophy. There was his father, Henry, seated on a gum stump just inside the orange glow between his two brothers. Jack was on his right hand leaning against a hackberry. Bob squatted to the left near the fire as he used a long haw pole to turn the crackling armadillos the clan had roasting for their hunting dogs.

Henry was handsome and had a magnetic personality. He was the Chiron of the Cut and Shoot students of physical culture. The swamp runners who spent their lives browsing through the thicket tangles in search of their razorback hogs invariably found their way back to the clearing alongside Henry's home. There they learned the arts of living a robust, practical life in tune with nature's concept of development of blood and muscle.

Roy had learned to be reasonable and be practical about the nature of things from his father. Night after night as Big Henry sat beside the fireplace rubbing his shotgun, he had told his sons of the shortcomings of mankind and of the pathway to Heaven. Henry had learned those lessons well, and from the hinter most fastness of the forest the sons of the woodsmen had been sent to sit in the informal lectures he delivered after sundown on the long front porch of his home.

While the whippoorwill called in the elm flats, Henry made his young disciples feel that God was real and near. He would point toward one of his wife's pot plants on the shelf near the water bucket and ask with the dignity of an Aristotle what made it grow. Then he would explain how the sun's rays governed its growing.

On a summer's night he would point to sheet lightning playing thunder-heads far to the east over the Trinity River and explain to the pupils on the porch that his pa had said it was caused by rays that were visible. But the whippoorwill's notes and the faint grumbles of thunder resulted from invisible waves rippling on the eardrums. His God was real as the moonbeams. He could talk with Him through the medium of brainwaves and through some unseen channel, the mind, which was part of God, could impart impressions to the soul-seat in the minds of others. Some call this mental telepathy, but because Henry never heard the expression, he called it horse sense.

From the gum stump, and by this time everyone around the chunk fire was sleepy, Henry asked Roe, in a yawning sort of way, about the limestone caves along the Arkansas River in which Spanish soldiers in the long ago had hid their gold.

Roe snorted through hooked nose hairs in a disgusted reply to the question.

"In there where John Wesley was raised along the Arkansas twist the Ozarks and the Ouachita's there was a heap o' talk 'bout Spanish gold buried in the foothills, but John Wesley did not pay aire attention to that gold talk. For most of his twenties, his whole life was took up with Indian Territory.

"He had gone into the Territory 'a fore the government had the land run and had found out what he wanted. He knew some other people who came down across from where Montague County, Texas is now. Their name was Tuckers and they had come to

Oklahoma early. John Wesley married a daughter of that family when the country was still Indian Territory. He sent her to Texas when he went to make the run just 'a fore the 19th century turned.

"Well, the gun fired at somewhere around noon that day as well as I can remember. Everybody made the run on horseback or in a wagon or buggy. Everybody was there by 8 o'clock 'cause they were camped all along the line of old Oklahoma in their wagons and tents just waitin' for the gun to shoot.

"John Wesley rode an Indian pony called Ben W. across the Territory of Oklahoma. He staked his claim across Little Bear Creek, then he went back and got his oxen, wagons, and Mrs. Harris, and Sybie, my wife, who was a baby then.

"He took his oxen and hooked them to a plow, a sod plow, and he broke up the sod and took a shovel and cut up that sod and made a sod house to live in. He had an old tent he had been livin' in at the startin' line and while he was breakin' up the sod for the sod house, Mrs. Harris and Sybie was livin' in the tent."

Roe paused for breath and took a swig of blackberry wine before he continued.

"He built that sod house two days after the run and he made an extra room out of the tent. He took some elm poles he got out of a holler and spread the tent over them. Then he pitched sod over the top. He lived in those two rooms nine years and worked that place and settled it and proved it up. He had a hundred sixty acres in his homestead, and Jack was borned in that sod house and growed up in the badlands.

"Later John Wesley took his wife and those two kids back to Texas, and Ben W. he died just this side of the Red River. They had just crossed the Red River when that horse took sick and died. They moved on to what was known as the Marsh Place on Keechi Creek in Anderson County, Texas."

It was getting late by the time Roe had recited the multitude of adventures encountered by the emigrant Harris's in Anderson County. Not only did he tell of the birth of Henry and Bob, but he would revert to the wild ways in Oklahoma where John Wesley had been a sage brush lawyer and a United States Marshall.

The legacy of John Wesley is very important to Roy as witnessed by the space to which he devoted the subject in his memoirs:

Our style of life during my childhood was much as it had been when John Wesley Harris moved his family to Cut and Shoot in 1912 from the Oklahoma Territory. My grandfather was a lawyer, a brilliant man who spoke 16 different languages, several of which were Indian dialects. There was much hunting, fishing and telling of stories of ancestors and family.

John Wesley Harris was born in Franklin County, Arkansas; Lida Tucker was born in Oklahoma. J.W. Harris and Lida rode in the last Cherokee Strip in Oklahoma in 1896,claiming and staking their claim and lived on the property until the acquired title was obtained. During the seven years they were there, they had three children who died. When they left Oklahoma, they dug up their three children and took them to Palestine, Anderson County, Texas and reburied them. One of the girls was less than one year old when they crossed the Red River. An old Indian tale was that any child that crossed the Red River less than one year of age would soon die, and it came true for them, as they buried her along with the others in Palestine.

They settled in Palestine where Henry was born. He was three years old when they moved to Conroe, Texas. Nine of the sixteen children lived to be adults and came to Conroe with their parents. They lived in the southeast portion of Conroe temporarily before moving to the Cut and Shoot area. John Wesley bought about 200 acres in the John A. Davis survey abstract 188 in Montgomery County, Texas.

John Wesley was a blacksmith worker and farmer; he also had several registered horses, cows, hogs and dogs. He felt like he wanted the best and thought that if the animal was registered, it was the best. He had a photographic memory and could quote most of the Bible without looking at it. He could sit at a railroad station and watch a train pull out and leave town and could write down each number on each boxcar in order by memory. Rumor had it that only two other people in the world could perform that feat.

His talents were varied. He drew a life size picture of his prized stallion, named Jolly Boy, and set it out by the road for people to see if they wanted to have their mares bred by the registered stallion. My dad recalled that if one of his registered animals became tangled in a rope, he would immediately cut the rope rather than take the chance that they might receive rope burns while was trying to untie them. My dad disagreed with his father and would allow the horse to work his own way out of the entanglement and would not cut the rope unless it was necessary to save the animal from severe injury. However, if his dad were nearby, he would cut quickly like his dad would do!

Among John Wesley's talents was a penchant for agricultural science. For instance, he had five different kinds of apples growing on the same apple tree through grafting.

The fire was low in its bank against the pin oak logs when Roe in his ramblings had reached the end of the year 1912. The thicket men knew the story from there on so they dozed while their minstrel wove his epic of the moving of John Wesley and his wife and children to Cut and Shoot. They were all asleep except

Roy, before Roe's narrative came to the part where its subjects reached the fringe of the forest they now called home.

Roy was uneasy so he interrupted his uncle to ask why anyone should have to fight alike a rooster in a cockpit and call it prize fighting.

Roe knew the lad was worried so he looked around the circle to be sure that everyone was asleep. Then he spoke softly as he passed by the boy on his way to his pallet.

"Your dad was a bare knuckle champion. All the Harris's are fighters so they expect you to be. Fact is you got to be, so you just as well be a good one or get clear of these woods, or let them worry wart you like a crow pesterin' a chicken hawk."

Roy was drowsy but unable to sleep. Far to the north he heard a wolf howl and farther to the north he faintly heard the pack answer. Suddenly the world seemed lonesome and primitive, and there at midnight amidst the wild sounds of the woodland, the fifteen-year-old youth figured out his formulas to cope with the future.

He remembered the sage logic of his father about the life span of man from the time of the cave dwellers down the millenniums to the present. He had heard him reason on the porch that physical fitness was simple to achieve if the one who strove for it paid attention to a few natural laws that were obvious.

Over the thousands of years that man shifted for himself, he rose early in the morning and waded through the primordial dew and swamp shallows in search of an animal or reptile he could conquer and devour to satiate the grumblings in his belly. Seldom did he secure his breakfast without engaging his quarry in strenuous combat for a brief period of time. Were he successful, he gorged himself on the choice chunks of the kill and dragged the remnant home to his family. Then the hunter sprawled on the floor of his cave in complete relaxation until hunger aroused him again to venture out for game.

Henry said people lived like that a million years before they got lazy and put food in cans. No wonder they are weak today, he would say, when they eat breakfast in bed and play games at times when they should be relaxing. Roy remembered his father stressing the fact that the Neanderthal man was strong as a plow horse simply because he unconsciously patterned his life to nature's plan of development.

Deep in the dreamy night, the young man foresaw his future. Roe had said he would be pestered like a chicken hawk if he scorned the mores of his people. He disliked to be pestered, so even though he longed to lead a gentle, contrite life like his mother, he resolved himself to answer the call of the wild life that his father advocated.

Roy reached his decision, much as had the Biblical Jacob on that memorial night when the angels climbed the ladder at Bethel. Jacob wanted to languish forever in the tent with his mother while the redheaded Esau, Like Tobe, roamed the fields with his father.

Roe had said that Tobe was more like his grandfather "than 'aire one of his kids or grandkids." Tobe was the huntsman, the philosopher. The Indian sign of his forebears was strongest upon him. It was ironic that while he slept, due to a mess of crow and chicken hawk tale served up from Roe, his birthright was slipping from him to his Jacob-like brother, Roy, wrestling on the other side of the fire with his conscience.

Like Jacob, Roy was destined to labor many years before he proved his worth by obtaining a world heavyweight championship fight. Before arriving at the precondition for securing that fight, that of a number three ranking among world heavyweights, Roy would have to follow the pattern of multitudes of his ancestors and always rise before the sun and splash himself with cold water. With skin and blood thus stimulated he must trot awhile, walk awhile, and run awhile, until he had ranged at least five miles before returning home.

In his memoirs, Roy describes his attitude toward training as follows:

A boxer who is preparing himself for a fight with an opponent, whom he expects to be in top shape at the time of the fight, needs to properly prepare his boxing condition for the entire length of the fight in case it does go the distance.

In preparing a boxer for a fight there are many things to consider. He needs to be in shape mentally for the battle. The boxer needs to avoid worrying about financial and family problems while preparing for the fight. Training for and winning the fight is the main goal. The boxer needs to enter the ring with boxing and winning being the only thing on his mind at the time.

A fighter needs to do the physical preparations by pushing his body to exert all the speed and power that he possesses. A fighter needs to do what is known as 'road work' in the boxing game. Roadwork is running, trotting, running backwards and any other work done on the road. A fighter needs to do his running on the road in the following manner. He should run slowly until he warms up while doing calisthenics. The fighter should then run at full speed for about ten seconds and then run at a fast speed for another twenty seconds and then at full speed for another ten seconds. This should be repeated for a total of three minutes and then walk fast for one minute. This procedure should be repeated for forty minutes. In the three minute blast the runner is simulating a flurry of blows he is delivering to an opponent.

I think that running, chinning, wrestling and lifting weights in the proper way adds to your ability to box. Learning to wrestle should be watched very carefully because it is easy for one wrestler to damage another wrestler permanently. If done correctly, wrestling is important to a boxer in infighting where two boxers are in a clinch. Knowing how to get out of the clinch without being injured is very important. A boxer should be very careful about lifting heavy weights without supervision.

It is very important to do all the necessary things that prepare a boxer to win his upcoming fight. Even if a fighter does all of the things that properly prepare him to be at his best condition and position to win, he still may lose the fight, especially in the heavyweight division, by being hit by one lucky punch. If a fighter is properly prepared, he still has a much better chance to avoid a lucky punch from his opponent.

This is where a good corner man is indispensable. A fighter needs someone in his corner that he can trust and who knows his abilities and disabilities. The fighter's corner man must be able to see anything that the fighter is doing that puts him in severe danger *and to make him aware that the opponent may try to attack him in that way. He must be able to look at the opponent and see the things that the fighter has done in the round before that helped him to beat the opponent. He should be able to tell what the opponent is trying to use on the fighter to win the fight and what can be done to avoid him doing so. A good corner man that knows a fighter and how he fights can make the difference in winning or losing.*

Lying there by the fireside with his kinsmen and friends, thoughts of how he must train whirled through Roy's young brain. Suddenly the whirling stopped and he saw clearly his course. It was simple and not to his liking but determination set in as in rigor mortis. Just before he closed his eyes, he saw his brother shift his red head in a sort of restless way on the tow sack as an alligator bellowed in the bay gall. His last waking thoughts were of Hominy lying there recuperating on the hard ground; he was happy that his friend was at least safely out of the company of the slimy crawlers of the slough.

Morning came up like thunder, because an Easter norther bore down in a cold, gleeful sort of way. The hunters wrapped up their bedding, and while the lightening played among the trees along the high banks, they bathed themselves in the warm waters of the river.

As they were hurrying to slip on their clothes, they saw Hominy crawl up to camp. He was haggard, and his face was drawn in a pitiful expression, which begged without speaking for another swig at the white oak keg. Bob gave it to him with a mixture of kerosene, which he had tied to his saddle skirts in case of snakebite.

Hominy thought he had been poisoned. He dragged himself down the riverbank to the edge of the water and after splashing himself in the river, he lay on a sandbar and moaned, "I never thought I would've died like I'm a dyin'."

Bob sat beside him and dared him to die. He spread his hands to the oncoming norther and solemnly preached his funeral.

"Hominy, you aren't a bit o'good to yourself. You aren't any good to me 'cept you can knock boar hog's tushes out better'n most folks can. 'Sides that you're a dang good well digger, but when you're a drinkin', your principles aren't any better'n a polecat. Go ahead and die. I always wanted to see somebody die who thought he was and wasn't."

Bob was real happy as he gave Hominy another swig and pulled him back up the riverbank. The norther had blown in with its swirling winds, which he knew would be a big help while he robbed a bee tree.

Bob got the honey and spilled and rubbed a large part of it over the unconscious Hominy. As soon as the norther passed, the sun came out to shine in a relentless baking way on the already blistered face of the hapless man. Bees began to swarm and settle over the still form of the honey-covered, moonshine-soaked hunter until he had the unearthly appearance of a corpse being subjected to hungry maggots.

The others were down the river rounding up a few straggling hogs. Bob left Hominy and joined them. Bob's brother, Jack, asked him about Hominy and laughed out loud when he found that his brother had missed his breakfast " 'a fooling around with Hominy!"

The north wind was stirring the pine needles up between the boles of the big loblollies and floating them across the right-of-way that belonged to the river. Armadillo had a pig he had taken at random and tied down in the saw briers, where he was inflicting a slash or two on its ears with his throwing knife

Jack rode up just in time to admonish him to think about what he was doing. "Take a long stern look at yourself, Armadillo," Jack warned, "Now if this isn't the last time I have to have this talk with you, you better be prepared for some big-time harsh consequences. You must be careful and respectful when you're unsure as to whether a pig is yours, not just 'hully-gully' grab anything that moves and go to work on it like you're a doin'."

Satisfied that his message was hitting home, Jack lightened up. Tapping Armadillo on the shoulders and smiling, he said, "'catch my drift there, ole partner?"

And catch it, Armadillo did. Never again was he to be seen confiscating a specimen of livestock at random without serious consideration of whether it was the rightful property of a fellow woodsman. When Jack said something, it was to be adhered to.

About the time that Jack finished his admonition to Armadillo, Hominy came up with his tongue hanging out, swearing vengeance on Bob and Jack and the entire world.

Thus was the life and world of the Harris's, their kinsmen, and their small smattering of neighbors in the wild woods of Cut and Shoot, Texas.

Jack was a tiger in a switch cane infested jungle. His life was raw. He loved to linger alone for weeks far out in the forest matching wits with the wolves. His trap lines extended from the West San Jacinto to the Trinity River. He loved to find hunters in the woods and pretend, in his most sincere way, that he was their pillar of fire by night, then put an alligator in the bed with one of them.

One night the complaining of a newly found acquaintance that had rheumatism disturbed his sleep, so he threw him bodily into a swirling river. Then, when he saw that the bewildered fellow couldn't swim, he jumped in and saved him. Jack was kind to those he completely trusted. He was gracious to all except his enemies and to those friends he singled out for his terrible practical jokes.

Sleep to Jack was sacred. Even Henry was loath to wake him when he had hunted long into the night without resting. If Henry left him alone, no one else dared disturb him. There were times during the Conroe Oil Boom when certain oil field roughnecks would come upon him dozing after a hard day's run on a deer trail. At those times his temper was short.

A blast or two on his hunting horn would bring his hound dogs on the run, and together they would make short work of the disturbers. Jack always had his roaring last laugh and an added emphasis was totaled to the tales of the merry "madman" who roamed the wilderness.

Jack was the oldest of John Wesley's three boys. He had been born in the days when his father was wending his way each morning from the Oklahoma sod house into a pioneer world built of logs and buffalo hides, chinked between the cracks with words dripping with backwoods wisdom and dusty sand.

Jack was wild and wise as he wandered through the hazy, rain-splashed fastness in which he found himself when his family moved to Cut and Shoot. He selected his friends from the honest, hard-working country folks in the area and molded them with ferocious sincerity into loyal followers. If they measured up to his standards, he would travel the darkest trail to their assistance. Most of his followers loved him for what he was, but some tagged along because they sought the protection he afforded them.

Chapter III

OIL AND CONFLICT IN THE 1930S

In the early 1930s, an edge of Cut and Shoot became the great Conroe Oil Field, named for the nearby town of that name. Almost overnight, the field rose to become the third largest in the United States. What had been animal trails through the canebrakes were widened into muddy wagon roads down which streamed the component parts of a thousand derricks.

The results of the great event were mixed. At the time, the once booming timber industry of the Conroe area was evidencing a steep decline, forcing the closure of many mills. In 1930, Conroe's only bank failed, generating financial doldrums across the land. Conroe's schools struggled to complete their terms. However, due to the great oil strike, by 1933, the Conroe area was evidencing a precipitous rise in its fortunes. The Conroe school district became one of the state's wealthiest, and for a brief time, Conroe claimed more millionaires per capita than any other town in the United States.

But there was another side to the story. In Conroe, itself, things became so dangerous that men were afraid for their women to leave home, especially during night hours. The dark side was, if anything, even darker in the midst of the oil field, itself. Allison Sanders of the Houston Press recorded a sampling of the impressions of the residents of the oil field area in March 1933. None of the parties interviewed were of the Harris clan, but were their neighbors and friends.

One of the respondents to Sander's survey responded thusly: "Doggone it, anyway . . . how come these fellers want to come in heah an' mess up Montgomery County this way? . . . It was a good country . . .The land would grow anything—after the trees cleared away. Now look at it. Spoiled."

Another respondent to Sander's survey observed, "They sure ruined this country for farmin'. " He then added, "I've got two producin' wells, one drillin', and another located on my land." However, he was yet disquieted: "but I'm figgerin' on movin' on somewhere else. . . .They've trampled over all my fields, broke down all my fences. Why 'fore these oil men came I had 300 head o' hogs runnin' through these woods . .

. .They've mostly been eatin' now." And, he added, "I reckon I didn't eat 'em."

So, along with men who were wealthy, down the rutted roads that the derricks made came hungry and desperate men from all over a nation deep in the clutches of a vast depression. Some were bona fide employees of oil companies who had been sent to do a job, but many were hangers-on and camp followers.

Tent cities sprang up on the low ridges in the swamps in which stealing and fighting and con games occupied the time of most of the inhabitants. Riffraff battled riffraff for a multitude of reasons. Often times brawls began without a reason because along with the legitimate workers employed as troubleshooters, came the troublemakers. Many of those loitering around the boom towns were looking for honest jobs in order to sustain families back home. Among these, were men weighted down with responsibility and disappointment, easy pawns in unscrupulous hands.

Some became craven fools after the big payoffs were in their ragged wallets. Those wallets contained pictures of wives and children left behind to hope and pray that their men would send for them later. Hence, each time their wallets unfolded to receive the wages of sin, conditions became more desperate. One foul deed climbed upon another to gain and conceal a dishonest dollar until all sense of decency dissipated. In the end theirs was a clouded, criminal conscience, or even worse, no conscience at all.

Still the ground shook to the screaming release of the subterranean gas pressure, followed by puking petroleum flowing in sickly green belches to long rows of battery tanks. The swamp was heaving up her gall from down deep in her gassy magma.

There were knolls that jellied when the intense gas pressure rose to the surface on the outside of the drilling casing. When those knolls plunged down hundreds of feet into the disturbed quick sands surrounding the viscera of the earth, the noise of the sinking was overpowering.

At times, the nauseating gas became inflamed. The resultant light encompassed the thicket glades where the hog hunters met and listened to Jack Harris, the "Tiger", prepare the doom for the foreigners prowling on his property.

"Henry," Jack insisted, "you're the settle'est one a-listenin', an' you know if our pa was here, the hoot owls would still be roostin' on Crater Hill 'stead of those 'town-boys' killin' all the grass an' a killin' hogs that don't belong to 'em. We aren't gonna have no rights any more if we keep watchin' 'em act like Santa Anna at the Alamo. Twixt now and in the morning we gotta drag some of 'em down here where we are now an' have a talk."

Cousin Coon Massey stood up when he saw Henry was still thinking. He had been standing near Bob, his inseparable and jolly companion. Whatever Coon said suited Bob and vice versa, unless it was in contradiction to the will of Henry. To give Henry time to think, Coon started talking.

"I 'spect that some of these folks need to have their necks stretched, but we need to abide by the law and try to avoid trouble. Henry and Jack will know how to handle these hog thieves. Other day I heard some of 'em say how mean we ought to be treated, and it made me feel awful bad to be so bad as they say. But I wasn't as bad as they said, so I don't feel so bad.

"Shucks, folks said I couldn't fence the trail in front of my house. I did. I said, if you don't think I'll fence it, you watch me. I said if I don't put a fence 'cross the trail, I don't know who is. Other day those boys came up the trail with an ox wagon full o' tools, and wouldn't you just know it, they up and cut my wire. I didn't have but one strand twixt the saplins, but they busted it.

In his memoirs, Roy relates the story of how Coon received the name by which he was known amongst the woodsmen of the forest green.

Coon Massey was nicknamed by Henry Harris. Arthur (his real name) would go down to Crystal and Caney Creek to catch fish. He would feel around under the banks in the roots of the trees and catch them by the gills. Henry said that he looked like a coon feeling for crawfish.

As the young men grew anxious to quell the boomers, Coon began to worry about Henry's hesitation to respond: "I hope Henry don't sit there all night and think. His pa, who is buried at Dry Creek Graveyard on Crater Hill, would fight. 'Bet that graveyard has caved in by now 'cause of all that oil drillin' and those city slickers have sent your pa a hunnerd miles straight down to where their oil comes from."

Henry had heard enough. He had a baby named Tobe at home in those terrible depression days, but when his father was mentioned and when a question of right or wrong needed to be settled, he could deliberate no longer. He didn't have to say much. The woodsmen were ready.

"We'll get 'em, but not tonight. I need time to think it out," Henry exclaimed.

Henry had been married to Gladys Murray on Christmas night three years before this evening of pivotal decision. Oil had been discovered before his honeymoon was over, and the thicket was being overrun with honest men and with thugs. He had been happy at home, content to bash in the faces of a few drunken derelicts that he had met along the trail. Now Coon's speech had changed all that. Fifty men in their twenties were in their saddles waiting for him to send them on a mission seeking frontier justice among the tents on the low ridges.

Roy's memoirs refer to his mother and father's wedding:

[They] married on Christmas Day in 1930, which was during the Great Depression. A young lady by the name of Gladys Eunice Murray came home from school with Helen, Henry's sister, to spend the night. Gladys lived in Conroe, and Henry was working, cutting timber in Navasota during the time they were courting. Henry would ride the horse to and from Conroe to visit Gladys, which was about 80 miles round trip. They courted for about a year and waited to marry until she finished high school, which she did by graduating early in December rather than in May of the following year.

A Conroe businessman, Dan Madeley, who went to school with Gladys said that she was the smartest person who ever went through the Conroe Schools. She had the highest grade of any student in her grade and would have been the valedictorian if the entirety of her school years had been spent at Conroe.

Gladys was born on October 9, 1912 and was the eldest of five children born to Andrew Jackson Murray and Una Blanche Pentecost. Her sister Marion was followed by a brother, Harry Joe Murray. Bob Murray was followed by the birth of baby Dorothy Wayne Murray.

Gladys was a fantastic cook and sang all the time. She was a good athlete, even after having nine children. She would run races, play hopscotch, marbles, tops and jump rope with us. She encouraged us to stay active with physical exercise. I remember her as being very pretty. Her hair was black as a raven's wing and remained that color until her death. Her teaching us to jump rope taught me timing for my boxing.

With thoughts of Gladys and the baby Tobe weighing heavily on his mind, Henry waxed cautious: "Now listen men. There's no use to fight a world full of money. These folks are here to make a livin'. Most of them are good and clean like a clear creek, and they have folks like we have. When your dogs run a 'possum in a holler log and you reach in and get your hands covered with pole cat musk you don't blame the 'possum. There are some real stinkers driftin' 'round these parts. They're the critters we're a lookin' for. I don't know who they might be. You don't either. Go home and Jack and I will figure out what to do. Meet here tomorrow night."

Henry spoke slowly. If his words had been more rapid, there would not have been enough time for the pulse of the young men to become quieted.

The hated noises of the drilling rigs could be heard pounding through the timber, and it nauseated the men in the glade. They hated the red glare in the heavens that was a reflection of ignited gas roaring hundreds of feet above the treetops. It sickened Henry too as he rode off in the direction of home. He had to pass one of the rigs on his way so he decided to ride up to the derrick floor just to check it out.

He dismounted in front of a red-faced man unloading cordwood for the boilers. "Where'd you get the wood you're haulin"?" Henry was a gentleman when he asked the question, even if he did feel that his liver sank because of it.

"Henry, you know where I got it!" Stuart James's red face flushed a little redder. He threw another pole on the pile by the boiler before he asked about Jack and Bob.

"Jack's all right and so's Bob and I didn't recognize you, Stuart. Let's talk out yonder away from all this racket!"

When they had reached a spot where ordinary conversation could be heard above the clanging drill stems, Henry asked Stuart if most, or just part of the boomers were no good.

"Henry," Stuart began, "You and Jack and Bob and me and a whole lot of others have watched this oil field from its beginnin'. Mr. George Strake sunk every penny he had to bring in the discovery well; he is a good Christian man who deserves every speck of oil he can bring to the surface. He and his company can't help it if punks come here to fuss and fight. You can't help it either. The best thing you boys can do is to do like I'm doin'. Get into the thing. Join up with them. There's plenty for everybody who wants to work."

Stuart paused to study the impression he had made on his friend. He added, as he tapped Henry on the shoulder before he started back to the cordwood pile, "We don't have to start anything, but we can sure finish any trouble these hangers-on want to kick up, can't we?"

Henry and Jack talked all the next day about what Stuart had said. They made several mysterious trips together over the old familiar trails talking to certain leaders among the woodsmen. They also were seen riding through the toughest sections of the tent towns, talking to thugs who seemed to have long since given up any semblance of decency they might once have possessed.

Jack left Henry late in the afternoon promising to meet him later in the evening in the glade.

That night almost every nester between the east and west forks of the San Jacinto River below the Willis to Coldsprings road who was old enough to set a steel trap, was waiting in the glade to hear what Henry had figured for them to do. They had brought saddlebags of extra ammunition because they had heard that Henry had been on the prowl since sun up with the Tiger. Surely they would have the fight they wanted, since Jack had been advising their leader.

The yells let loose by the milling Cut and Shooters when Henry rode up, drowned, for the moment, the ever- lasting humming and whining of the hated drilling rigs.

"Let's string 'em up tonight," some of them shouted. Some cracked their long bull whips while they hollered. No one knew what to expect since their leader was so unpredictable. They had hoped that the rebellious fire in Jack's disposition would kindle and quicken the deliberate and calm spirit of his brother.

"Listen, men!" Henry said it in a crisp way that shocked like a wolf's bark. After he said it, he reined Old Mutt, his powerful blood bay horse, to the center of the small meadow. Old Mutt reared up until his forefeet sparred with right and left jabs as he danced on his hind feet in a tiny little circle.

The woodsmen became silent before the awful spectacle of the youth flouncing his glossy black whiskers to the racing rhythm of his studhorse. They felt their own horseflesh quivering beneath their saddles. Perhaps the horses felt the men in the saddle shake. At any rate, a hundred livings things, counting men and mounts, were awed by the black-headed man on the strong red stallion who was demanding their attention.

"This mornin', before daylight, I had a talk with Jack. He talked like you talked last night. That's the way I felt when I left you. On the way home, I spoke to a friend of mine who is your friend, too. I told Jack this mornin' what he said. Now listen. We are gonna fight, but we are gonna do it so we don't hurt anybody that's aimin' to do right."

Henry had been their leader since John Wesley died in 1928. Henry was approaching his nineteenth birthday when he helped dig his father's grave at the foot of Crater Hill. Since that time the wild, calloused men of the swamp had followed him. Some of them remembered the young man and his brothers digging their father's grave. The boys had told them that their father had just waded over the swamp into the briers on the other side.

They had seen them take John Wesley in a buggy down the sandy hill to the grave they had dug and, after a Christian ceremony, lower him into it with buggy reins. Since that time they looked to Henry for advice even though Jack was the oldest. Now that young man was weakening. Jack wouldn't weaken, they thought. But where was he?

"Where's Jack?" somebody shouted. The impatient men in the clearing repeated the cry. Coon tried to quiet them.

"If you think the East River's not full o' gars, go look! Those 'gars 'er worser than all the mess here abouts, but the East River keeps a flowin'. 'Hit's a gonna eddy into the sand banks and knock the cocklebur patches in the bottoms clear down to the ocean. These boomers are like cockleburs. They're sure up to no good. We'uns can try to dig 'em up by the roots as if they were palmettos. I say, let 'em wash down the river with the cockleburs."

Coon didn't know what he said, but he accomplished his purpose, giving Jack time to get into the opening. The Tiger signaled in the gas lit glade for silence.

"I'm startin' a slush pit gang in a few days. We are gonna dig slush pits for the drillin' rigs. Henry and I went out today among the folks a-drillin' these holes an' they told us there aren't enough slush pits. You all know that they need big tanks so's they can have water to pour down the holes they're diggin' so's it will be soft enough to dig in.

"We went clear down among the no account folks livin' in 'boomer town.' Lots of 'em wants to work for us. Henry and I picked the biggest an' meanest ones to join up with us. We're gonna have a tent town of our own and we're gonna abide by the law. We've been here longer'n anybody and we have a right to build a tent town if we want to, just the same, and more 'so than them.

Everybody was listening except Coon. He was looking at Jack and admiring him. That's all he cared about. It made no difference to him what the Tiger said just so Coon could look on in admiration when he said it. He knew that John Wesley was wise, knew the law, and had taught his sons well.

Jack was hammering out details with the men: "I want you to bring your teams to the flat on the south side of Dry Creek graveyard three days from now. That'll give Henry and me time to get some slips to dig with. Bring along the same amount of grub you would take on a two-week's hog hunt. That will give us time to get tents to live and to cook in and get all around set up. Anybody have somethin' to say?"

Everybody was thinking, so the night was still and quiet except for the hated clang of the oil field machinery pounding in echoes from the red glare hanging over them like Satan's halo. The steady unnerving sound nailed wild decisions into their brains. Jack waited for the re-borning.

"Go home for now," Jack said. "We'll think on a plan of justice in as civilized a nature as we can muster under these conditions." Then from the depths of his inner being came a roar reflective of his namesake, the Tiger.

The re-borning was complete, for with that fiendish wail the woodsmen humped up and howled, venting their frustrations. The night swelled with modern racket from the derricks which, when mixed with the wails of the woodsmen, seemed to echo from ghastly banshees on an ancient moon lit heath.

Though burdened with the trials of the newborn oppression, as these weary woodsmen headed for home their tempers were calmed, for the moment, with hope of a solution without bloodshed. Having for the time being redirected the angry woodsmen's energy in a positive direction, the Harris boys traveled while pondering the details of a plan of action. The brutal assaults and lootings, which the interloping thugs had been inflicting upon the native woodsman, must be addressed, but, if possible, in a manner which would not turn the woodsmen into the same mindless hordes as their adversaries. Sought was a strategy that would bring safety to their homes, their wives and their children, while preserving the dignity that was their birthright.

Chapter IV

WOODSMEN VERSUS BOOMERS, ROUND 1

Sixty men were on the payroll during the boom of the teaming camp's heyday. They were a motley lot. Besides the native sons of the swamplands, there were those, such as Roy Tipton, Jim Ware, Silas Nobles and Treetop Combs, who drifted out into the world again to become notorious in their own rights.

Roy Tipton became Henry's fast and loyal friend. They rode side by side, with their reins in their teeth, against the squalid squatters. Together with the Tiger, they kept busy devising lawful ways and means to deal with the thugs and cutthroats.

During those forays through the forest, a second son was born to Henry and Gladys. They named him Roy after Roy Tipton. In his memoirs, Roy tells the story of his birth, how it took near miraculous conditions to save his life:

My story almost began and ended on the same day. On June 29, 1933, Gladys Murray Harris began to have labor pains. She sent my dad, Henry, to get his sister, Aunt Mary or his mother, Lida Harris, to come and help her because she believed that I would be born soon. Mary arrived riding behind my dad on his horse and began getting ready for my birth.

After quite a while, Mary realized that I was trying to come out feet first, a breech baby. She began working to get me turned around; it was a long, hard and arduous task, but she finally managed it. By this time, the labor pains had ceased. She had my dad bring in a bucket of cold water and began putting cold towels on my mom's belly. The labor pains started again. After I was finally born, I was not breathing and was blue, as I had been deprived of oxygen for a longtime. She dipped me in warm water and then in cold water and finally got me breathing, and all of the phlegm out of my lungs.

Thank God for the blessing of having an experienced midwife who knew what to do to turn me and get the labor pains started again. Otherwise, I doubt if I would be here now to tell my story. I found out later that I was her 65th baby to successfully deliver. I think that God had a work for me to do here on earth. I have always tried to be honest and fair in all of my dealings with others and tried to help when prompted by the Spirit to do so.

In the volatile atmosphere surrounding Roy's birth, the denizens of Cut and Shoot built a fence around their teaming camp to make it private property. They allowed only members of their select band on the inside. From time to time, a deputy sheriff appeared with a warrant for someone's arrest. The woodsmen though knew from hard experience that many times a warrant was based on trumped up charges from some silver-tongued boomer. Therefore there was an inevitable bantering of words at the gate to allow the culprit, should he be known to be innocent, to slip under the back fence to fade into the forest that he knew so well.

Jack, the Tiger, wore a brace of six-shooters low on his hips. They were always kept in good repair with new ammunition in the cylinders just in case some upstart disputed his authority. His hat was curled upward at the sides and sat cockily on his head. If he had stuck a feather in it and leaned against a greenwood tree without the pistols, a literate dreamer could have imagined that he had seen Robin Hood.

During the day they worked with their slips in the rotted dirt to scoop scars that would hold water in the stinking earth. At night the men sought to stay at home protecting their families. But it wasn't easy, for sometimes the boomers would block the paths to their homes and even stoop so low as to terrorize their wives and children. It was then that in self-defense, it was necessary for the woodsmen to maneuver in roving bunches through the boomtowns in search of those who had wronged them. And woe be unto those who had tried to violate a woodsman's home, should the perpetrators of the dastardly deed be apprehended.

The woodsmen at times became so frustrated that remarks like the following were common: "My huntin' dog got tired 'cause the oil folks breathed up all the fresh air."

Suffering such frustration in their immediate environs, when the men received a rare opportunity for some clean adventure outside of the shaded greenwood, they grabbed it, with gusto.

At those times of attempted reverie, Bob was the clown prince of the Tiger's court. He sat at the head of the table in the mess tent and washed down huge gulps of venison while contemplating some audacious but friendly prank or adventure. He would even on occasion work his happy-go-lucky way through the enemy ranks giving everybody a hearty greeting, while contemplating their character traits for psychological weaknesses which could be exploited should a future situation demand it. If he had to be constantly on guard against those enemies, he would find a way to enjoy the battles.

Being single, Bob liked to have fun in the evenings after work whether the boomers were involved or not. A for instance was late one evening when he was on his way to Spring Creek for some whiskey with a friend. They puttered through Conroe in a T Model Ford with the motor hissing. As they were passing through, they saw a tent-show on the edge of town with a huge elephant staked out behind the tent.

"Law me, what a big rubber cow!" Bob exclaimed.

His friend, Thomas Caldwell, said he was not a cow, but a rubber bull, and the argument started.

Bob told the story later: "Old elephant was standin' up there weavin' like a snake, you know. We didn't stop 'cause we didn't have any refreshments yet, so we went down to Ed Morton's place at Spring Creek and come back and I bought 'bout two or three dollars' worth of peanuts, and I went around there and started feedin' the poor old elephant peanuts. Thomas passed over and asks the ol' elephant if he is a he or if he is a she-- 'cause it is night now. We had bet on whether he was really a he or not.

"Well, ol' elephant took his foot and knocked Thomas's feet from under him and started walkin' down his leg. I had already fed him all my goobers by that time so he put his nose down and commenced feelin' 'round my leg. I said, 'well, I believe you are feelin' for some more goobers, ol' buddy, but you're fooled 'cause I don't have nary 'nothern. You don' swallowed some of the packages even!' He put a suck on the side of my leg with about half wrap on it and picked me up, and I'm here to tell you, I got handsomely frightened when he started up in the air with me.

"About that time he kicked Thomas over and started mashin' him with his hind foot. I thought I'd punch my finger in his eyes to make him turn me loose so's I could run off. But he wouldn't let me punch him in the eyes. He just kept dwadlin' me right on up in the air and I kept wigglin' around on one leg.

"To 'reckly he said 'Phewt!' There was a whole bunch of kids out there, little ol' bitty kids lookin' at ol' elephant. He spewed me right out there amongst those kids 'bout twenty-five or thirty feet. I lit just like a flyin' squirrel spread out there on the ground; but I lit backwards, flying squirrel usually lights frontwards. Since it hadn't hurt me a bit in the world, I jumped up quick, and Thomas came a-draggin' his leg. The kids took off like they were a goin' somewhere.

"Thomas said, 'I got a 30-30. I'm gonna kill me a elephant.' I said, 'if you don't have a bigger gun than that you better get on a race horse when you shoot.'

"I walked back over there to ol' elephant and was gonna scold him. I didn't think the ol' thing could reach me. Next thing I knew I was hollerin' for Thomas to get me down, but he was layin' down out there with all the meat mashed off the bone of his leg laughin' at me. Ol' elephant said, 'Phewt," again, and I sprawled beside of Thomas. By then I must tell you gentlemen, I had had enough of that mammy of all the jungle creatures. So I said calf-rope, let's go to the hospital and quit messin' with the ol' thing. He's a bad cow, if he's not a bull anyway"

Still the battle of the boomers and the woodsmen raged. Jack gave orders that his men were not to steal under any circumstances. They promised, then some went out and robbed whomsoever they pleased. The Harris boys could not control all the men laden with justifiable anger in their hearts. Consequently, they sometimes suffered the blame for deeds they were trying to prevent. The pent up frustration of their followers on occasion prompted fights in the camp, when there was no one to fight on the outside.

The following story illustrates the Harris boy's view of stealing by their own employees: "On one occasion four men came back to camp drunk and bragging that they had stolen some items from the boomers. They said that the boomers were afraid to pursue them when they left because they had told them that Jack Harris and his men were waiting nearby and would string them up if they pursued them. This story was quickly relayed to Jack because everyone knew that the Harris boys didn't allow any stealing because it violated their moral code. The men were escorted back to the place where they stole the items. They returned them to the boomers, admitting that the Harris's had nothing to do with the stealing."

Jack told the boomers that anyone caught stealing was not acting on his behalf. He added, "We will fight to defend our homes, families and property, but we are not going to steal anything. We are not thieves!"

"Needless to say, the men who stole were fired and told never to come near the woodsmen again."

In spite of the Harris boy's noble efforts to bring peace, finally someone summoned the Texas Rangers to see what they could do about the anger seething in the Conroe Oil Field. Finding it difficult to sort out the claims and counterclaims of the woodsmen versus the boomers, they apprehended both Bob and Henry, along with a host of the boomers.

When the Rangers departed, a few unscrupulous lawmen had the brothers placed in separate cells in the Conroe jail with nine of the "boom boys" with Henry and thirteen with Bob. Henry and Bob had been unjustly arrested and thrown into jail with angry boomers bent on their destruction. Then from the lawmen came instructions to try the Harris boys in kangaroo court. Naturally the verdict was guilty. The penalty was thirty lashes to be administered to Bob and Henry in their separate cells from the hands of the boomers.

Little did the lawmen understand the peril they were inflicting upon their benefactors, the boomers.

When Henry was grown, he was six foot two and a half inches tall and weighed 225 pounds. He had black curly hair, extremely good eyesight and good teeth without any rotten or missing even when he died in his 80s. He was very fast with hands and feet and was well developed physically because of his hard work around the farm and in the timberwork in the area at the time. He learned to ride and break horses and how to work and drive cattle to different places in the area.

As he grew up he wrestled with his brothers, and he boxed different people or neighbors in that area. He learned how to box from Matt Bruton and his brother, Jabe "Duke" Bruton, along with several other boxers who worked in that area during the time Henry grew up. Henry had an extra-long reach and large fingers and hands and was one of the best heavyweights ever to box here on earth. In his prime of life, probably no man could have whipped him in a fair fight. He told most people that he had never been whipped by anyone except his father, and his father took the cowardly advantage of him and made him bend over and back up while he whipped him.

Henry boxed for an oil company and traveled to Louisiana to fight opponents. They even brought a world champion wrestler out in the oil field to wrestle Henry; Henry threw him two times, and he hit at Henry on the 3rd wrestling round, and Henry hit him and knocked him out.

Roy continued on another occasion, adding further details on Henry's athletic prowess:

Henry was extremely fast; he raced when he was in the Coast Guard and usually won. He was the fastest runner in the 100 yard dash and the one mile run. While he was in the military, he began boxing and continued throughout his years of service. When he got out of the military and came home, he began to work in the oilfield, which had begun to develop into a huge industry in East Texas. The timber business was beginning to fade away when the "black gold arrived."

He continued to box with other oilfield workers that were working in the oil industry at that time. Some of the wealthier oil people who were aware of Henry's fighting ability brought in other boxers from other oilfield camps in Texas and Louisiana to fight Henry. He whipped the heavyweight champion of the South (Ed Dunaway) and all of the other top fighters in the area that would fight him. He knocked Dunaway out *in the 4th round in the first match and knocked him out in the 2nd round in a rematch.*

He would either box or wrestle with them, as he was good at both. The promoters tried to get him to go to New York to fight Joe Louis, the reigning world champion at that time. He declined saying, "I won't go to New York to fight him, but if you bring Joe Louis here, I will be glad to whip him!"

Now that same Henry Harris, a man with dynamite in his veins, stood cornered, assessing the kangaroo court decision at the hands of the boomers. Then quickly Henry knocked down five of his would-be floggers before, under the sheer weight of overpowering numbers, he fell upon a woodpile. Upon realizing this was a streak of good fortune, he first quickly praised the Lord for placing him in a position to save his life. Then he seized a piece of the stove wood and went to work like a raging bull. He cracked skulls and arm bones all around him. Blood ran from a dozen gashes and flowed to thick red puddles on the ground. Henry was fighting for his life.

Henry was a young man protecting himself from a gang of boomers with a stick of stove wood, and he didn't cease his flailing until he had the un clobbered ones at bay against the cell wall. Around him lay the mangled broken bodies of men who badly needed a doctor. A battered Henry, numb to the point of paralysis, stood precariously in the center of the cell.

The lawmen summoned Doctor Ingram but Henry met him at the gate and dared him to enter. Thinking he was going to die anyhow, Henry didn't want the others to live either. Besides, he suspected that this was just a way to throw him off guard so the boomers could catch him and beat him to death.

In the other cell, Bob was down, and around him lay the foolish men who were responsible. Only a few were still able to stagger around and beg for medical attention. Henry told the doctor that he would hunt him all over the world if he went into Bob's cell and helped the man who had killed his brother, for he thought they had killed Bob. Bewildered at the awesome scene, the doctor hesitated, unsure of what to do.

Suddenly, up the street strode Jack with his pearl-handled pistols loose in their holsters. Men began to move back along the boardwalk because they could see scores of horsemen, followers of Jack, standing their mounts at the other end of the street from where Jack had come.

The Tiger walked up to the scene of the action and, in a disdainful manner, motioned for the deputies to unlock Bob's cell. He went in and slung the limp body of Bob over his shoulder. Then he disgustedly walked through the lawmen to a wagon that one of his teamsters had driven into town. Upon placing Bob gently in the wagon bed he turned to examine Henry, all the while looking in a baleful way at the boomers. Later, after investigation by the proper authorities, it was found that the charges against Bob and Henry were bogus.

Bob was convalescent for weeks. He sat on the banks of Crystal Creek and fished most of the time. When he felt better, he wandered off hunting to exercise himself back into shape. He believed that a change of scenery would help his condition so he hunted over towards his friend, Booger Morgan's, shack. Morgan told him the Rangers were back on the prowl and were watching him pretty closely. Bob thought it was time for some fun so he told Booger Morgan to come go hunting with him and act like they were going to camp out.

"We will leave before sunup", he said, " 'pack our dogs and stuff in the back of my T-Model, and we'll go campin' down on Peach Creek."

They had started out down the road with the dogs in the back when they saw a buzzard sitting on a limb of a dead pine snag. When the buzzard flew from the limb and sailed down the road toward them, Bob got worried.

"We were just this side of the Fire Look Out when the buzzard saw us and came a sailin' down the right-away toward us. I just raised up my automatic shotgun and with a bunch of number four buckshot fired on him and here he came. He was one of those black popular jobs and 'ker-plunk', he lit right between Booger and me at seventy-two miles an hour. I couldn't dodge, and Booger couldn't dodge. He was drivin' down the ol' sand road, and he slunk over as for as he could and I slunk over as far as I could and ol' buzzard come 'ker splash, 'right between us and liked to knocked the back seat out. Those ol' hounds sittin' up in the back let out a howl 'cause he ricocheted and knocked two of 'em out of the car. We had lots of fun, but one of the hounds died with a buzzard bone through his throat."

Finally making his way back to camp, Bob told Cousin Coon his buzzard story. Slapping his hands with an "Oh lawdy," Coon went berserk with laughter. In his inimitable way, he told the whole training camp.

"Now, gentlemen's, Bob ought to feel lucky he didn't get plumb kilt by that buzzard. The most powerfulest thing on earth is a half gallon of oats fed to a donkey. Now gentlemen's, that is power. I saw a donkey eat half-gallon o' oats early of a mornin' and plow all day in sodded ground. It was dry and wrung out ground too. Misters, that donkey never missed nary a step.

"I hear tell of folks nowadays who break fresh ground with tractors. A half gallon o' gasoline won't get one of them contraption's motors started of a cold mornin', let alone enable 'em to plow all day on it. I say half gallon o' oats fed to a donkey is the most powerfulest thing on earth. A buzzard flyin' out of a tree at seventy two miles an hour though is right up near top place, and, gentlemen's, Bob tangled with one. He's bound to have a lot of nerve, else he's crazy. I think he's plumb crazy."

Like all the citizens of Cut and Shoot, Roy was impressed with Coon and enjoyed the way he purposely tortured the English language at times to make telling points in his stories. Roy tells a story reflecting Coon's ingenuity way back when he was just a child:

Coon was probably a full-blood German. His father spoke nothing but German, and Coon never learned to speak English until he was five or six years old. Coon used to tell a story about a teacher who went to the bathroom in the old outside toilet, which was a two-holer. Coon was upset with the teacher about something that she had done. When she went to the outdoor toilet and closed the door, Coon went to the back of the toilet and pushed it over on its door. The teacher could not get out through the door and had to crawl out through one of the holes. As one would expect, the chagrined teacher inflicted upon Coon a good whipping with some small limbs from a nearby tree. Coon was twelve or thirteen years old at the time.

Coon was from a large family. He eventually received some royalty from an oil company when oil and gas was being produced in the Conroe Oil Fields. The Massey family owned land that was located in the edge of the Conroe Oil Fields. Others took most of the money illegally, which the Massey family should have received. They did receive free gas from an oil company while residing on the old Massey homestead.

Bob's episode with the buzzard had Coon wound up. He was on a roll, telling stories, letting his imagination fly:

"Asides from bein' the next most powerfulest thing on earth to a half gallon of oats, a buzzard dive-bombing a car is the next nervest thing what is existin'. But the most nerve, gentlemen's, is generally found in a red-boned hound dog. The biggest red bonded hound I ever did have the rapture o' seein' was a hand span wide cross the shoulders. Now then, you good men won't believe me, but late last fall I was in there 'bout the gravel shoals on the west San Jacinto River, behind the ol' Herrin place.

"The Foley boys were in there in hog camp and they had caught a 'enormous size bobcat and had him in a coop made out of rattan. They had a red-bone, the likes of which the Good Lord has never expected to see, tied to a tree. With a certainty it would ah took a two-handed man to span his shoulders. Just for fun, I cut the rope close up to the collar. Next thing that ol' dog had his nose clear up to his eyeballs 'tween them rattan bars, and was a diggin' with his hind foots to push his way in. The coop just slid long the ground.

"The cat, he was a big 'un. He stood up on his hind legs like a boxer and ripped that red-bone's nose with his front foots. If ever you see a winchester bullet a shootin' through the air, and I doubt if any o' you gentlemen's ever did, you could write her up as bein' 'bout as fast as that ol' cat. If she was as big as me and wore boxin' gloves, she would win the world's championship in every round.

"I had fun what was slap-dab funny. Them Foley boys was maddern a unwrapped package on a Christmas evening. Ol' red-bone wasn't even gettin' uncertain 'bout quitin'. I knowed his face was a mess and gettin' messer and messer. I tell you, gentlemen's, a red-boned hound, two spans 'cross his shoulders got nerve. We had to take his hind foots and drag him out o' there.

"Wasn't no chance for him to live, bein' cut slap to pieces. He'd look sad at the coop, then at us. We knew what that dyin' ol' red-bone wanted so we turned the cat out.

"Sirs and gentlemen's, did ever you see a cat catch a mice?

"Let me assure that a red-boned hound dog is the mammy of any kind of nerve what is born on this earth. Next to him ranks in second placed a buzzard divin' into a car at seventy two miles an hour."

Finally having his fill of Coon's lesson on power, Henry turned from the rest of the camp workers and walked away. It was just in time to see Bob hop his horse and lope out of the gate in a cloud of dust. Worried, since Bob was yet recovering from his big battle with the boomers, Henry asked Roe if he knew where Bob was going.

"I expect he's goin' to Lynx Thicket. I overheard him tell Jack that was the best place for him to go to exercise himself and get well."

Henry had heard of Lynx Thicket. It was way down close to where the two forks of the San Jacinto come together. He also knew that today some people called it Tasserly Thicket because Tom Tasserly had stayed in those jungles and killed several men and gambled and robbed. Tasserly was an outlaw in the old days when his pa was living. Henry was concerned that there might be some of the old outlaw gang still hanging out in those wilds.

Everybody had thought Tasserly was wealthy. Henry knew better because he had talked to Old Man Madison, who was Tasserly's best friend. Old Man Madison told him that Tasserly had counted out twenty-four hundred dollars the morning he was killed and had given it to a woman with whom he was staying to keep. Nevertheless, a legend grew up about the assumed riches of Tasserly that were supposed to have been buried in Lynx Thicket.

Suspecting that hog thieves yet made their home down there and knowing that Bob wasn't afraid of anyone, but was still weak from his recent brawl, Henry hunted up Roy Tipton.

"Roy," Henry began, "Bob has gone into Lynx Thicket to get himself well, a huntin' and fishin'. We'd better tail him. I'm thinkin' that those hog thieves down there are gonna give him plenty of trouble."

The second day out they followed Bob's tracks into trouble that could only be dreamed up by Lucifer, himself. This excursion was to be the beginning of the end of Roy Tipton.

Not taking into consideration the boldness of the merry Bob, they had no idea he would ride directly into a stranger's camp without first checking out his surroundings. They followed where the tracks led and suddenly found themselves within a couple of yards of the muzzles of three machine guns. They had never seen weapons like that before.

"What kinda gun is that?" Tipton asked Henry.

"They're machine guns" Henry replied.

A boyish-faced man commanded them to dismount. He ushered them into a tent where they saw Bob sitting at ease in a canvas backed chair. A woman held a little pistol on him with a cigarette in her mouth. She was as relaxed as Bob. She stood up and politely offered her chair when Henry and Tipton walked in ahead of the gunmen. Bob grinned at the woman.

"Looks like you gonna get your rain barrel full o 'us wiggle-tails," Bob said in his innocent, and what he hoped, disarming manner. "We' are just a rainin ' out of Cut and Shoot. Henry did you bring the whole camp with you?"

Before Henry could answer, the boyish looking young man asked them to be seated.

"We are just hunters looking for deer," the young man explained. "There's no place like around here to find them. Only bad thing," he continued, "is the unfriendly folks you meet. They come in here occasionally and want trouble."

"We came down here to see if Bob is okay," Henry replied as he looked around for signs to prove that the man had told the truth about being a deer hunter. "We are from up country a ways, do hog huntin' and team work in the Conroe oilfield. Name's Harris. This is Roy Tipton. Sorry to be of trouble to you folks."

He still had seen no signs to prove they were deer hunters.

The woman and two men seemed to take Henry's word. They told them to make themselves comfortable, but never troubled to introduce themselves. They spent the afternoon with them. Towards evening Bob and Henry received permission to leave. But they had taken a liking to the boyish-faced man and the liking was mutual.

Tipton had a fever so he remained for a while longer with the other man and the cigarette-smoking woman. The Harris boys did their best to persuade him to return with them, but he was determined to stay where he was until he recovered. That was the last time they ever saw the good looking Roy Tipton who had ridden down the many trails of adventure with them.

Henry and Bob returned to the Dry Creek Teaming Camp. A few days later, as they were nearing Henry's home, they came upon the makings of a camp. Stopping to take stock of the situation, suddenly appearing in their midst was the now familiar boyish face of the machine gun totting gentleman and his entourage who had just recently held them captive.

"So soon we meet again," spoke up Henry, surprised to see them so near his own home.

"We camped here for a short while because we knew you were on the outs with these boomer people, 'figgered you wouldn't give us any trouble." As an afterthought, he continued, "By the way, your friend, Roy Tipton, is doing fine. He went up north with some friends of ours who joined us after you left."

Henry could no longer restrain himself. He thought that if these people had the audacity to set up camp so close to his family, he had the right to finally insist on ascertaining their name. When Henry asked, the boyish faced man yet again deflected the question, seeking instead to focus Henry's attention to clarifying a story of local legend.

Henry hesitated, his curiosity even more ignited as to who the stranger might be, but again decided the better part of valor lay with letting the matter rest, for the time-being. He then consented to the man's request to address the saga behind the local legend.

"Yes," Henry began, "so the tale goes, when the Mexicans were on the run from the victorious Texans after the Battle of San Jacinto, down toward the coast, they were scrambling through here, and saw a nice spot to bury their gold. Ol' timers say it was right here, about this bend in Crystal Creek."

"Thanks for the confirmation," said the winsome stranger. "If we happen upon the treasure, we'll let you know."

Never receiving such notice, it is assumed that the gold yet remains buried in that sandy loam down by the creek. But Henry learned later that something just as exciting as buried treasure had been his experience. The baby-faced man to whom he related the story was none other than the celebrated fugitive from justice, "Pretty Boy Floyd."

Tom Tasserly, "Pretty Boy" Floyd, and Roy Tipton: What fascinating tales the tangled hearts of Cut and Shoot and Lynx Thicket hold. There are tales of buried gold, of desperate men on the dodge and of hog thieves waking in the night when dry twigs crack for fear the authorities are coming to hold them accountable for their dastardly deeds.

The only bit of merriment in the Lynx Thicket's heart is the memory of the day when Bob Harris entered it. With a song on his lips, he rode boldly up to the outlaw's camp into the very noses of their sputter guns.

"I sure am hungry, strangers," he said. "If you have any strippings in the meat box, I'd be obliged to light and eat. Now don't you folks worry none 'bout me, 'cause a rough lookin ol' piney woods rooter like me sure couldn't be 'Pretty Boy Floyd.'"

There was a bit of merriment in "Pretty Boy" Floyd's heart too, when he cocked his machine gun and told Bob to get down from his horse. "Reckon you couldn't be Jesse James or one of the Harris boys from Cut and Shoot?"

Chapter V

WOODSMEN VERSUS BOOMERS, ROUND 2

The Infant Roy in a Fighting World

It was 5 o'clock on Sunday, December 13, 1931 that the George W. Strake No. 1 South Texas Development Company location gave forth, in guttural grumbles, the first petroleum to reward the faith and long suffering of that location's namesake. Just 2400 feet away, on June 5, 1932, Strake brought in a second and even greater well that catapulted Conroe into the national limelight as a premier oil field.

Strake had persevered to prove to the world that the battery of scoffers had been wrong in their contentions that he should drill west of the San Jacinto River, instead of to the east in the flatlands where the sea in the Pliocene Age had its shores. His story, like that of Louis Pasteur, was one of absolute reckoning where in the savor was the salt of common sense.

People as far away as Bombay, India knew about the discovery before the natives in the Big Thicket learned of it.

It was during that pivotal year of 1932 that a major oil-related catastrophe occurred very near the Harris home. Roy tells the story of Crater Hill:

Crater Hill was a part of the Conroe Oil Field and about one mile from the Harris home. In 1932, there was an explosion of an oilrig there owned by Standard of Kansas. The explosion blew pipe into the air high enough so that some of the pipe landed more than a mile from the explosion site. Millions of gallons of oil filled the crater.

Crystal Creek ran through one of the craters. At that time there were no regulations of how to control the explosion. The creek was dammed up and much of the oil was collected by tankers and taken to the nearest refinery and sold. No effort was made at first to stop the well from flowing.

The public demanded that something be done. I have been told that the Crater Hill project was the first directional drilling drilled into a well that was blowing out. The directional well pumped heavy mud into the blowout well and eventually enough was pumped in to seal off the blowout well. The oil and gas could then be diverted to come out under control through the pipes.

The well had run wild for 45 days before it could be controlled.

A man attempting to burn waste oil that had accumulated lit a match which ignited the gas in the air. The wind was blowing the gas from the well toward the man when he struck the match and the explosion happened. Instantly, the fire killed him. Sand that was blown out of the well by the high pressure gas was carried by the wind over five miles away to near Conroe. This fire continued to burn for a long time.

The two initial Strake wells coupled to incidents such as the Crater Hill fiasco turned gas and oil and confusion loose in the adjoining thicket, and in this setting Roy Harris was born.

It was eight-thirty after the summer sun had set behind a golden bank of rained out clouds that Roy came to his mother and father in the cool rain forest. Uncle Bob called him Robert. His father called him Roy for his friend, Roy Tipton. Thus it was proclaimed to the world on the following morning, June 29, 1933 that Roy Robert Harris had entered the world and was at home to all visitors with his parents in Cut and Shoot.

Tobe was a sitting-alone-baby, having been born only sixteen months before on March 3, 1932. This was not quite three months after the first Strake well came in.

Uncle Jack rode up to have a look at the baby Roy. He had ridden from Conroe that morning, after appearing in court as a character witness for a friend.

"Do you know the accused?" the prosecuting attorney had asked.

"I do," was Jack's reply.

"What does he do for a living?" the attorney continued.

"Well sir," began Jack, "he raises some hogs, makes a little bootleg whiskey, and dynamites the river when he's hungry for rockfish. Besides that he's a constitutional man with a good family that needs his support and can hardly get along without it. I can talk fair and truthful for him. I say turn him loose."

The jury had been composed of frank men like Jack. They loved the truth, and they respected Jack, so they had rendered a verdict of "Not Guilty," making it possible for the man whose character Jack had lauded so highly to go home to his dependent family.

Luke Ferrell happened by while Jack was scrutinizing the baby.

"Well, Luke, what do you think of my nephew?" was Jack's purring question to Ferrell.

"He's bound to be born in shape. That's the way every Harris I ever heard of is born. He won't have to climb trees and knock the bark off his knees to muscle up. They all been born in shape."

Bob went out to the barn supposedly to feed his mare, but he came back with an earthen jug from which he poured four tin cups full of reddish liquid. He offered one to Henry, one to Ferrell, one to Jack, and kept one for himself which he raised to the level of his eyes in a toast to the new-born baby:

"Here's to the newborn baby,

and to his father, straight and tall.

May he grow up to be a man someday,

that exceeds us one and all."

They tossed off the toast while, between the cries of the babies, they heard the wails of the oil wells surging and fading in the morning breeze. There was work to be done by the men in the slush-pits. Then they most probably would have to fight their way in the evenings through the ever-tormenting waves of boomers who blocked the roads attempting to deny them passage home.

Roy grew up behind his brother. He crawled along the wooden floor of the cabin and put his fingers in the holes in the log walls made by recent boomer's bullets. He grinned at the giants who came though the doorway because they were friendly and occasionally lifted him into their laps.

One of the earliest recollections of Tobe and Roy was the night their Uncle Bob came home and barred the door. He sat in the darkness at the window waiting, with his shotgun, for someone. The boys pretended to be asleep, but late in the night they heard the dogs bark.

They cannot remember too much because they were so young, but they do remember their mother loading an extra shotgun and handing it to their uncle. They can still imagine they heard the hoof-beats of many horses pounding in the darkness and that their daddy came bursting into their bedroom after Bob opened the door, and gathered them into his strong arms.

Then they heard their father say, "Bob, we must go to Four Corners."

Four Corners, where the chain of events leading to the scene at the Harris home that night began, was so named because it reminded most folks of the four corners of the flaming underworld. It was the high seat on which sat those with the worms of malice working in their hearts. Bob had been there earlier that evening just to relax and dance to the tune of "Sally Gooden." He had ridden to the Corners on a fine-blooded mare he had left tied to a stake out front. After the dance he found that four drifters had decided to take turns about riding his horse. That made him "ferocious mad", sending him into a sort of rage.

"I don't hardly believe you'll need to ride my horse!" he flared with his nostrils open as wide as he could flare them. Bob loved his horse and cared for her as a mother would care for her newborn baby.

When he looked at his horse's flanks and saw they had roweled her until the hide was split in crimson gashes, he was beside himself with fury. The part of his brain that contained destruction snapped clear down to the bedrock to release a seething torrent of anger into his rushing bloodstream.

Foolishly, the drifters, thinking they had numbers on their side, attacked. That was a most unfortunate mistake, for Bob began to sing:

"Lay down your burden down by the riverside,

'cause you ain't gonna ride my mare no more."

Under Bob's fighting fury and singing rhythm, four went down, needing medical attention, while the other two managed to slip through to the metropolitan tent area where the bums played poker far into the night for greasy chips that were worthless. Here they stirred up a hanging party seeking to flush the troublesome Bob from his forest haunts and swing him to a tree limb.

Roy remembers part of the particulars of that night. Tobe remembers most of them. What stands out clearly in both boys' minds is seeing the gang of men that had come to the Harris home in the dark of night to kill the Harris family later fleeing on horseback into the darkness from whence they came.

Tobe and Roy were growing up in an area over run with rough and rowdy boomers filled with lust and greed. They could see, through their infant eyes, hurt caused by men devoid of conscious who had interrupted the harmony of a once peaceful community. They watched and learned that the law does not always protect the innocent.

The cabin in which they lived was actually four square rooms of pine logs. A long front gallery ran north and south on the east side to provide a place for relaxation and gathering for family activity, conversation, singing and entertaining guests.

Skilled craftsmen had framed the cabin to perfection; John Wesley had trained the craftsmen to maintain a standard of perfection in all things. The log walls looked up in hand-hewn plies to a sealed roof pitched at an ideal slope to unburden itself of the driving rainstorms belching forever out of the Gulf of Mexico. The windows and doors had no screens.

"The whole, wide world is invited to my home," Henry frequently remarked. Guests are welcome so long as they behave themselves and obey the laws of God. The yard was spacious. To the left was a fish pond supplied with water from a well operated on a natural gas jet. The pond was a ways from the house and extended northward in a shallow swamp with lowlands fingering out from the forest.

To the right the land sloped to the south to Little Crystal Creek. That quicksand stream curved to the west about a quarter of a mile behind the house spreading its valley in a panorama of light green willow sprouts. Farther west, up the hill out of the valley, tall magnolias stood to darken the clearing when the evening sun slanted low before it slipped beneath the foliage.

The sand strip directly in front of the porch where the road ran up to the house was the children's playground. Most any kind of improvised gymnastic equipment was there. A motor block served as a dumbbell along with a blacksmith anvil.

Gladys and Henry lived in a house they built on Crystal Creek. The house was later moved and an oil well was drilled where the house sat. They later built in the John A. Davis survey, about a quarter of a mile north of the oil well. They stayed there until a bigger house was built later. Henry and Claude Lang worked on building the new house at night by the light of the fire from Crater Hill. They later moved an old house from Henry's mother's place and attached it to the existing house to make more room for the children. They lived there and raised eight children, four boys and four girls.

Roy elaborated some on the connection of the house moving to the maneuvering of some of the oil dealers:

The house where I was born was moved later about one-fourth of a mile so that an oil well could be drilled at that location. The oil people divided the land into 4-40 acre tracts that were within the area where the oil was supposed to be. All four wells proved to be good; two of them were much better than the other two. Lida (Ma) Harris (Henry's mother) sold her mineral right to oil thieves who took advantage of an old, uneducated countrywoman. John Wesley (Henry's father) died before the oil boom came to the Cut and Shoot area.

Henry sat on the porch beside Gladys and motivated the boys to grow stronger and stronger as they strove with each other in the clearing. Henry came home every evening after work to sit in philosophical council with his children. Usually the porch was crowded with boys and their fathers from the whole countryside. Among the topics he discussed was the nature of the Conroe oil boom.

"They tell me in town that this oil boom isn't like the rest. I mean like Batson and Spindle Top and some of the others. The reason, they say, is those other fields let the boomers come in and take over. We haven't done that. The crazies came in here and tried it, but they haven't had the same lame reception like in those other boom town areas."

"Some of the law officers kinda let us folks down at the teamin' camp take up for ourselves, 'cause they had trouble with those drifters in other oil fields. They are, so I hear, thankful that we stand up and fight for our rights. Jack is glad the officers think that way. He believes in justice even though he doesn't have much love for some of those ham-stringing laws that have been forced upon us.

"The law may not always be right, but the law is the law and we must follow it. However, we don't have to take anything off those sorry folks that come down here stealing our livestock, insulting our women and acting like the world owes them a living.

"I bet a hatful of huckleberries that if one of those worthless land jumpers living in the tent towns were to die and go to that place below reserved for the heathens, he would break a leg trying' to steal somethin' on the way down there."

Henry would look out across the treetops where there was a little afterglow in the heavens. His ears would tune into the pulsating throbs of the derricks reverberating with sounds resembling a grandfather's clock alarming at three in the morning. Some of his audience of woodsmen sat in deerskin bottom chairs leaning back against the long wall, listening intensely.

The boys grew up in the wilderness. They learned the names of all the trees that grew in the big thicket. Their mother permitted them to hunt through the underbrush for snakes. Their father organized a "snake-killing good time" to thin out the snake population in the area surrounding the house to decrease the chances of snake bite.

When Tobe was six and Roy was five, they were with their Uncle Jack on the Trinity River. Jack had a trot line in the eddy waters of the river baited for catfish. The boat had been carried by high water on down the river. There was no way to run the lines unless the boys ignored the danger of the hooks and swam out in the deep water to take the fish that were hooked.

Jack sat on the sandbar and watched his trusting little nephews swim into the rapids.

Tobe treaded the water to the middle of the trot line. It was dragging downstream and toward the bottom from the weight and pull of something heavy tugging one of the hooks.

"Here is a big 'un," Tobe called to his five-year-old brother who was dog-paddling among the sharp hooks just above him. Then Tobe saw that it was a baby alligator about two feet long. He was overjoyed. The trotline was forgotten until he had fashioned a secure place for his newly acquired pet.

In a litany about what he did for entertainment as a kid, Roy relates:

Our entertainment consisted of what we could find to do outdoors and boxing. We had no organized sports until we went to school. I remember the first movie picture I ever saw. We rode on horseback to Grangerland where someone had brought in a big tent to town and was showing the movie in a tent. We played hide and seek with other neighbor kids; needless to say, we had lots of good places to hide in the woods. We raced each other and played chase or tag.

We played with non-poisonous snakes and alligators. I can remember two occasions when Tobe tossed a snake at me but can't remember why. Guess it was just part of how we played. We always had dogs, and we used them when we went hunting, which we did often for sport and for food.

When I first started to school, I would walk down a trail through the woods to Ma's (Henry's mother) house and catch the school bus there. I liked to catch snakes on the way to catch the bus. One day, I decided to catch several snakes as there were so many available. I wanted to show them to my friends on the school bus and at school. I had a wonderful bus driver named Johnny Freeman. He encouraged me to kill all of the snakes that I had caught instead of bringing them on the bus.

Though Roy was very much at home in the presence of snakes at that early age, there was one thing that, at that time, surprisingly rendered him uneasy.

One of my first memories of school was what I saw from the school bus. It was a huge building like the courthouse. I got off the bus, and the teacher told us to go inside to a big room, an auditorium. The teacher took me in to find a seat. There were many empty seats, but the teacher took me over and sat me down by a GIRL! I was scared. I had never been around a girl before, except my sisters at home. I remember the teachers there as being kind to me. They seemed to know that I was scared.

Tobe, like his forefathers, loved the wolf calls at sundown. He loved the sound of the alligators splashing in the deep blue river lakes. Roy loved those sounds also, but he simply took them for granted. Deep in his young mind he felt sorry for the eight-foot alligator gars that arched so beautifully out of the waters. "Why?" he thought, "Can't they have the opportunity to do something better?"

He loved to hear the wolves howl. They sounded restful after a long hunt in the forest during a steaming afternoon. Still he pitied the wolves because he felt that they had been relegated to an insignificant role in the great drama of life acted upon the stage of the world. Roy also pitied any animals whose habitat had been disrupted by people who had no regard for the ecology of nature.

Wildman and Armadillo were a few years older than Tobe and Roy. No common family blood flowed in their veins, but there was a collusion of kinship that made its mark on them due primarily to common interests and a long-standing feeling of interdependence of their elders upon one another. Wildman lived down the road about three miles from the Harris's. Armadillo lived closer but the drilling crews on crater Hill were between them. Coon lived in a thicket below Armadillo.

One day when Roy was twelve a goodly number of the clan were on the long front porch at Henry's. An evening breeze was swirling and sighing through the pine trees south of the cabin. It gusted up to the porch to dry the perspiration dripping from the foreheads of those leaning in siesta in deerskin bottomed chairs against the porch wall of the log house listening intently to Henry tell stories of former times. It was close to six o'clock p.m.

Henry reminded Tobe and Roy to get their homework done. He repeated his often spoken regard for a good education. "The more you have, the more you will be able to help others. A good education will help you achieve that."

"Henry's right," said Tobe as he and Roy headed into the house to study at the huge kitchen table. Tobe and Roy respected their dad. He was always good to them. They knew that he loved his family more than anything and that he wanted the best for them.

The great respect Roy had for his dad.

During World War II, I would get up at daylight and feed, saddle and bridle two horses. I would then ride with my dad to a nearby community called Four Corners, where Henry caught a truck to go to his work in the oilfield. After he left, I would ride my horse, leading his, back home, unsaddle them and put them in the pasture for the day. I would go through the same procedure in the evening meeting Dad at 5:00 when he got off work. As I always carried my 22 rifle with me, we would often shoot one or more squirrels along the way and would eat them for supper later. My dad and I became very close during this time, as I had him to myself. He would also tell me interesting things that happened at work or stories about his childhood. He always had a story to tell.

While Tobe and Roy were studying in the house, outside the crickets sang and the spring-frogs croaked. Uncle Bob sat on the long dark porch and reminisced about his schooldays.

"I went to school a few days when I was a kid. Never was a schoolteacher taught me how to catch a 'possum out of a hole or smoke a rabbit down, or nothin'. I could build just a little bit of fire, put some pine straw on it, and make a rabbit drop right out of there. A teacher wouldn't tell me nothin' like that. I always wanted to study about somethin' to eat and there sure were no books that ever looked good enough for me to eat. I don't recollect all the names of my teachers. One was a long, skinny lady. One had squinty eyes what made you think she wasn't lookin' at you when she was.

"I went to some more teachers, Miss Sally Shannon and to Falvey Stephenson, but Henry said I wasn't in Falvey's class on account he taught the big kids. I thought 'cause I was big, I was in his class, but Henry said I was a big boy with the little ones."

Coon thoroughly enjoyed Bob's story. They had gone to school together in their younger days, so the things that were said made sense to him.

"Bob," he said, "you recollect that teacher we had at Ben Milam School that took us every day down to Caney Creek at dinner time to teach us how to be so nice and clean that the germs wouldn't get in our lunch? He used to look long in the face like a horse while we would wash our bare faces. I thought he was the smartest teacher I ever had. Never had but two though; the other was a woman who was awful powerful pretty. He married her. That is why I thought he had more sense than any teacher I ever had."

Henry was quiet. His thoughts were down the porch and around the corner with his boys. He thought about the role he had played in the drama written for the woodsmen by the sordid people who converged on the oil fields for illicit gain.

In this mood of reverie, Henry told his guests the story of "the great oath." He recalled that in June 1937, when his first daughter was born, he surprised the world of Cut and Shoot with a grand announcement. He vowed, "I won't drink another drop of moonshine or any kind of alcohol again. You folks might say I'm crazy, but I really mean it. I don't want my children to drink. I want them to set a good example for their children. Nothing good can come of drinking."

That daughter born in 1937 was named Helen. By that time, Henry had sired two sons, Tobe and Roy. But this was different. A precious little girl was now to be the blessing of his household. It was on learning that he was to have a daughter that he swore the great oath heard round the forest. Tonight, feeling an especially heavy responsibility to educate his family, though he had never violated the original, Henry renewed the pledge he made those ten years ago.

"By the eternal gods," he began, "I pledge again to one and all spirits and humans alike, that I will continue to abstain; I won't ever drink another drop of moonshine nor any kind of alcohol again."

When Henry had made his original oath, a shudder of disbelief had overwhelmed the whole greenwood. Uncle Bob had fallen off the porch that night, laughing. But tonight, there was calm. Indeed, there were even heard voices saying 'yeah yeah'.

Everyone there knew that before the original great oath, Henry had made his own whiskey since he was a boy. They remembered hearing about the time he had been raided by the county sheriff when the complete still had been carried into the swamps with the exception of the copper coil. The sheriff and his deputies had ransacked the premises for evidence and had the directing wisdom of Henry's Aunt Laura as they went about their job. She had sat, in her mother-hubbard dress, on a stump in the thicket glade and, in her gracious way, had tried to be ever so helpful. She had sympathized with them when they left, then gathered her skirts from the coils and went into the house.

They remembered another time when officers found the still and summoned Henry to appear in court. He carried his father, John Wesley Harris, along as his attorney.

"The still you think you have for evidence is no still," John Wesley proclaimed in a voice like thunder muttering from a distant summer storm. "'It is nothing but a bunch of junk. Sure, you might say, the thing is a still because it has everything a still has, that is, everything but one piece of copper pipe. I say, in the name of justice, where is that piece of pipe because, that is no still. If you look close, it is a strong-born coffee pot we use when the relations come to stay a while. A miscarriage of justice has been done by well-meaning paid officials. I say, since they are well-meaning and paid, that they should escort the strong-born coffee pot to where it was before they got it and leave it alone—with all due apologies for a grave miscarriage of justice."

The judge looked at John Wesley a long, long time as though he were taking a time exposure mental picture of a wise attorney to pass on to his grandchildren. "Not Guilty," he ruled, as the gavel fell in an awesome sound on the bench of justice.

"The Court orders that the coffee pot be taken back and replaced in the place of its finding. Case closed! Next case."

My dad, as a teenager during the prohibition years, had a liquor-still operating in his dad's blacksmith's shop. The revenue agents came to investigate. Before the agents got to look at the alcohol making apparatus, Henry's older brother, Bob Harris, took the coil and the dome off the still and took them out in the cornfield where they became lost. Ma broke the only jar of whiskey in the pantry, and the whiskey ran through the cracks of the floor onto the ground underneath. One of the agents smelled the whiskey and when called to testify in court, he said that he smelled the alcohol in the pantry.

John Wesley asked him if he had tested any of the liquid to determine its alcohol contents, and he said, "No, but I know whiskey when I smell it!" John Wesley replied, "My law books do not have any place in them that say that Frank Porter's nose could be used to determine the percentage of alcohol in a liquid." The Judge replied, "If I go exactly by the law, I could not convict anyone." John Wesley told him that he demanded the judge go exactly by the law with him. The case was dismissed. Without a coil or dome, the apparatus in the Harris blacksmith shop could not be used to produce alcohol. John Wesley required the revenuers to take the apparatus that they had removed back to the shop and set it up like it was before they took it away as evidence.

Henry walked down the porch to a place of vantage where the boys could be seen hard at their studies. When he had his fill of looking, he walked back into the midst of his kinsmen. Standing there, the moon glistening in his face, Henry made an announcement; to be sure that everyone remembered his message:

"Now listen up and remember this!" he said sternly. "Smoke all you want, and drink, but offer my boys or girls a drink of alcohol and you will have to answer to me. Now tell that all over Cut and Shoot. My children are gonna study and amount to something."

By the time Henry finished his message and sat down, Wildman Woodman had walked over to visit. Wildman was in Conroe Junior High and on this particular night should have been at home at his studies. However, until the renewed great oath rent the air, he had never thought at any given length of time on the matter of studying. Now it behooved him to ease into the room where the Tobe and Roy were

110

hard at work. Since his books had been left at school, he reached for a book lying near Roy.

The book was *Les Misérables*, by Victor Hugo. Upon receiving Roy's permission, Wildman took the book and opened it. On the fly-leaf was written John Wesley Harris, Franklin County, Arkansas, 1882. He opened the book about halfway and began to read. For a few minutes he continued the half-hearted undertaking, all the while scuffling his feet like an uninterested school boy. Suddenly he finished reading a paragraph that intrigued him. He read it again; then hurried to the porch with the lamp in his hand. Tobe and Roy, left without a light, hurried down the gallery behind him.

"Henry, look what this Hugo person said in his book that belonged to your pa." Wildman had put the lamp on the water shelf so he could use both hands to hold the book.

"I heard you and Jack and Bob talk about your pa a good lot of times. Seems like I knew him, but he died before I was born. But Mr. Hugo must have known him 'cause it seems to say so here in the book."

Wildman began to read to the assembled backwoodsmen, Hugo's description of Cornet the builder of barricade St. Antonio.

"He was a man of tall statue; he had broad shoulders, a red face, a muscular arm, a bold heart, a loyal soul, a sincere and terrible eye. Intrepid." Wildman began to stammer over the last word and some of the succeeding ones, "energetic, irascible, stormy, the most cordial of men, the most formidable of warriors." He slammed the book closed and waited for Henry's reaction.

Henry reached for the book, studied the antique binding, and opened the flap to the flyleaf.

"Don't expect pa ever knew Mr. Hugo," he said, "but if he wasn't describing pa, that Count was a dead ringer for him. But just in case he was talkin' about pa we ought to do somethin' nice for him." He paused to grin at Wildman.

"What's your complete name, young man?" he asked the boy.

Campbell Woodman, was the answer. It was given in as gracious a manner as the boy could give to hide his chagrin that Henry didn't recall that he had already been dubbed "Wildman" as a badge of honor for his prowess at fighting.

"From this day forth," commanded the monarch of the Big Thicket from his throne on the gallery, your middle name is Victor for the fellow that wrote that book. He didn't look close enough in the light to see that Victor Hugo's new namesake was a bit confused, trying to determine whether he should be pleased or chagrined.

Sensing the young man's mood, Henry patted Wildman on the back, seeking to reassure him: "I expect that my pa would be glad to know that a fine young lad in Cut and Shoot was named for his friend, if chance be, Mr. Hugo was his friend."

Henry had to have a certain amount of fun before bedtime, or bedtime would be postponed until he had it.

The name stuck and so did the great oath he swore. The Harris lads continued to study each night at the kitchen table and both grew up to be gentlemen and scholars.

Chapter VI

THE INDIAN HILL MONSTER

In the dim, gray dawn of Indian occupation in Texas, the Great Spirit located the Bidai tribe in a well- defined area that extended from north to south between Bedias and Spring Creeks, and from east to west between the Trinity and Brazos Rivers. This was practically the same territory that encompassed the original Montgomery County when it was organized in 1837.

For centuries before the white man came, the Bidai had lived somewhat unmolested behind the natural fortifications afforded by the steep banks of the two great rivers with their tribal strength concentrated to the north along Bedias Creek. Then, too, in that day, the Sioux had not driven the Comanche's southward, nor were the beach-combing Karankawas on the coastal plains to the south energetic enough to fight.

Furthermore, the wilderness eastward across the Trinity was the domain of the humble and friendly Tejas. The only danger to the Bidai in those distant centuries was in their southeast quadrant where their territory overlapped that of one of the Attacapan tribes called Orquoquisac.

Some authorities claim the Bidai were of the Attacapan stock and thus were at peace with the Orquoquisac because of their blood relationship. There is little basis for this hypothesis, especially when one considers that the Bidai were aboriginal in the area. By comparison, the Attacapan were latecomers even though they did possess the lower reaches of the Trinity and San Jacinto Rivers for hundreds of years.

The startling truth is that there was little peace that existed in those early days between the two tribes. The overwhelming evidence points to battles by the hundreds fought along the high banks of the rivers and on the timbered ridges between them. Today that no man's land of long ago is called Cut and Shoot.

The southern reach of the Bidai tribe was Spring Creek. When the Spaniards came they named it Santa Rosa River; that creek flowed eastward into the San Jacinto. The confluence of the two streams was claimed as the southeastern boundary of the Bidai. Thence, they claimed, their eastern boundary followed the east fork to its source. From the springs at the top of the river, their boundary line became imaginary and indefinite as it climbed the intervening divide to a point on the Trinity somewhere above the mouth of Bedias Creek. It was at the mouth of that creek that they built their capital city. Later the Spaniards called it Bucareli. Here the bottomlands are level and flat for many square miles, making a pleasant contrast to the high, uplifted hills in the background. It was from those hills that Chief Thomas, the greatest of the Bidai chieftains, governed his people.

To the southeast, the Orquoquisac made their inroads. They were a weaker tribe, and their blunt into Bidai land wasn't big. It was big enough, however, to conquer three Bidai towns of defense. When the Spaniards came they found one of those towns on the San Jacinto, a gunshot away from a place they later named Santa Rosa de Alcázar, under the rule of an Orquoquisac chieftain named Canos. Another Orquoquisac village under El Gordo, the fat, was on a high knoll at the junction of Spring Creek with the San Jacinto River. Up the river about a league was the strongest outpost of the Orquoquisac, and the wise and noble Mateo lorded over it.

Mateo's village was on a hill, about two hundred yards from the river. The hill sloped abruptly to a fourteen-acre lake averaging eight feet in depth. The village was built in the early days of the Bidai, much as that tribe had built Bucareli on the hill, to the north, overlooking a lake of similar size. By the time Roy Harris came along, Mateo's lake was called Carter's Lake, but its owner was Barley McComb, a family friend of the Harris's.

Historians have read the ragged records written by Joaquin de Orobio who led the first Spanish expeditions into this region, and, because Orobio found the Orquoquisac in peaceful possession, have assumed it was ever thus. Later some scholar, for some vague reason, supposed the two tribes to be kinsmen. It was easy then for historians to imagine the tribes living harmoniously together as brothers with common interests.

They forgot the caliber and stature of the chieftains that Orobio found among both tribes. Those wise counselors of the camp fires had brought their savage followers to the realization of the futility of warfare over a corner of disputed dominion, no matter who their rightful owner might be, that was rent with rivulets bearing stagnant waters, unwholesome for an Indian to live in.

The historians further forgot that these same chieftains turned their people to a lucrative trade with the French merchants filtering toward them from Louisiana. And lastly, they have forgotten that the land itself tells a story. It is there to read and the things to be read are written in bold clear letters upon the face of the earth and just beneath the surface. Historians leave such records to be read by archeologists, but so far, not many of them have attempted to read them.

While Henry and his clansmen looked for swine in the undergrowth, Roy liked to look a little lower for Indian artifacts. He became acquainted with the different glazes on pieces of pottery he found. An arrowhead found at a certain depth might correspond with one similarly shaped in another corner of the forest with the same kind of earth covering it.

He ordered books to study the mysteries of Indian archaeology. Tobe was interested in the romantic side of his brother's archaeological pursuits but the scientific angle held no ecstasy that he could enjoy. When he became bored with his brother, and the dead things he poked for in the loamy soil, he would interest himself in the squealing boar hogs that his father was marking.

Roy was particularly enthralled when the hog hunts led to Carter's Lake. The tales he had heard from Uncle Roe about the oval body of water were many and strange. The clan had hogs in the vicinity of the lake so they frequently visited in the area. On such visits, they usually made camp on the high knoll on its southern bank, the site of Mateo's Village.

Roy had a big box of assorted findings from the knoll at home with labels on them, but Tobe wasn't interested in the things lying scattered about the hill. His curiosity carried him each time he camped on its crown down into the limpid waters of the lake. The sounds of splashing things in the after dark intrigued him.

At night when Tobe was rolled in a quilt in the dewy grass with his chilled feet pointing to the lake and a cold moon riding the southern sky behind him, his thoughts were attuned to the night noises in the lake. On the other hand, Roy, bundled beside him, wondered at the spear points in the ground beneath.

One evening Berkley McComb rode over the brow of the hill to join the woodsmen on Carter's Lake. Roy was nine and Tobe was ten. Late that evening they roasted a shoat over the coals raking from a log-heaped fire. An evening meal in the making sent its essence curling on the slow air current down the curvature of the hill and into the forest. The fragrance slid up the nostrils of the many timber wolves lurking beyond the emerging dark curtain pulled down by twilight's after gloaming and tantalized them into howling at its goodness.

As night hurried from the east to join them, the woodsmen talked of many things. The Harris lads kept their ears open while their elders spoke. Curiosity was part of their inheritance which they could spend as they pleased, especially since Roy's interest in Indian signs was "just a-borning" and Tobe was already challenging nature to unlock its secrets. Darkness had fallen over the lower things of the forest when Tobe began to beg Berkley to drain the lake. At first no one paid attention to his supplications, until they became monotonous. Then Coon declaimed the camp into silence.

"Now see here, Tobe," he began. "That lake is plum full o 'gar fish. It's got a divinely delicious amount of other atrocious burgers a sittin' in the mud on the bottom with tushes longern' a Caney Creek boar hog's, and mind you, young fella', they aren't settin' there a brushing' 'em with town toothpaste for Sunday School neither. They are down there lookin' ugly for the general purpose to get at a body with meat on his bones. You don't want to be a midnight snack for any of those golly-monsters in the lake."

Berkley began, however, to get an idea. He had thought for some time, but not too profoundly, of pumping the water from the lake into the river so he could see what manner of creatures the lake contained. If he had any other reason for the pumping project, it never rose to the surface of his brain. Now that Coon had painted such a vivid picture of what lay beneath those murky waters, Berkley's curiosity was again aroused. When he told the clansmen in the floating hours before midnight of his plan, Coon brandished his verbal weapons.

"That water hole down there," he pointed his hand in the firelight, "is a well o' reptiles. I bet some of 'em got stingers on their tails longern' a horse doctor's needle."

Tobe broke out of his quilt roll like an insect bursting its pupa. He sat straight up and opened his mouth as though his tongue were a hearing organ. He knew he wasn't dreaming the good things he heard. If Roy heard them it was only a dream, because he was fast asleep.

A week later a tremendous centrifugal pump was whirling the lake water through an eight inch pipe into the river. A levee had been spaded into the saddle through which the rising river usually broke into the lake. Now the lake was gushing over the artificial hump, homeward to the river, leaving the slimy things it had mothered swimming in a shallow stagnant sea covering a deeper sea of mud.

The first suck was taken in early morning by the suction hose. Late that afternoon the duck potato roots in the western shallows stood naked beneath their bending stems. As the water receded, the wet banks showed gashes in their sides into and out of which slid alligators.

Tobe sat on a cypress log and watched them in amazement. Just before dark, during bull-bat playing time, a monstrous reptile oozed slowly from a dripping rent in the bank directly across the lake from where he sat. Forever, so thought the youth, the giant lizard from another age, wriggled foot after foot of his scaly body from the crack until at long last the tip of this tail whipped foam in the stinking lake.

Even though he was only ten, Tobe was wise to the ways of the wilderness, and no one knew better than he the ways most of the crawling things of the lake would wend themselves through the night to the river, just as sea gulls fly inland when the barometric pressure drops before a gale.

"What a dream," thought the red headed and passionate youth, to have such a specimen as a playmate back home. "Yes, oh what a dream."

Alligators were predators to all of our animals, including us human beings. There were gators in our lake near our home, which covered about four to five acres, and was about five feet deep in the deepest part. We dug the lake by moving the dirt out and making a dam; we used the antique method of a horse or mule pulling a slip (a tool to move dirt, similar to the front end loader on a tractor) that we loaded with mud and dirt from the bottom of the lake or pond while it was dry. The horse would drag the dirt in the slip, and it would be dumped on the dam to make the dam higher in order to hold more water.

The lake needed to be kept deep so the water would remain cool enough for the fish to live and survive. We had natural gas that we used to jet water out of the ground into the pond to keep it full. There were alligators that lived in our pond and were free to forage for their food in the woods, creeks and ponds close by. Due to the then recent passing of the stock law requiring that all animals be fenced, we kept our hogs in hog-proof fences which were near the pond.

Many hogs lived in the fence that covered or surrounded the lake, and the hogs would go down a dam that was across the water. This gave the alligators a great opportunity to catch the hogs as they were crossing the dam; the gators would pick a small hog (called a shoat and weighed about 40 pounds) and eat him before they would try and tackle a full grown hog and would not touch a grown boar hog (400-500 pounds) unless they were extremely hungry. The smaller hogs were easier to catch and kill and swallow than a grown one. The alligators were dangerous by being able to hurt any animal of any size. They can jump their full length in order to catch their prey.

The gator would be in the lake, completely under water except for the eyes. He would start swimming fast; the water would move showing his speed. He would jump toward land and catch the hog in his mouth. The hog would be killed immediately, but the gator would drag the hog into the water and turn over and over, making sure the hog was dead. He would then crush the animal in his teeth. If the hog were too big to swallow whole, he would bite off chunks and eat a bit at a time. We lost many hogs in this manner, but we had a lot of hogs.

I remember when a gator tried to eat me. I was walking by the dam on the pond and I had a 2x4 in my hand about six feet long. The alligator jumped out of the water making a big splash. I saw him coming and was ready for him; I hit him in the head as he jumped out of the water toward me. He immediately retreated and left me alone. My dad was watching from the porch at our home, and saw the water splash. He was afraid that the gator had grabbed me, and he yelled out asking if the gator had eaten me. I told him, "Not this time. He wanted me for his supper, but I changed his mind."

When Tobe was a teenager, he caught a really huge alligator. We kept it on display tied by a chain, 50 to 100 feet long, around his neck and to a tree for a long time. He was the largest alligator that Tobe was able to find in the United States after making phone calls to all of the zoos to find out how large their largest gator was. The alligator was 14 feet and 3 inches long. He offered to give this gator to a zoo, but none wanted this particular one, he was a strong, thick built gator.

Tobe caught the gator in a lake belonging to Albert Moorhead called Crews Lake, a natural lake near the San Jacinto River south of Cut and Shoot. On the night that Tobe caught the gator, we had left him there by himself.

It is at this point that we separate fact from legend, for some of the old timers had earlier told the story that Roy was with Tobe when this particular gator was corralled. But Roy says those were only rumors and that Tobe actually acted alone.

Hear Roy's side of the story:

On the night that Tobe caught the alligator, we had left him there (at Crews Lake) by himself. The rumor got around that I was with him when he caught the gator, but he was by himself. I was at home with my dad. He went there that night to catch a gator and his goal was to catch "the big one."

He had been hunting all his life and knew what to do to catch a gator. He got in a flat bottom boat and went onto the lake. He said that it was a moonlight night, but he was able to see well using a carbide light. He said that he could see many alligator's eyes. He was looking for the one with eyes farthest apart, as he knew it would be the largest gator in the lake. When he found the one he wanted, he waited for it to charge toward the light, and he dropped the noose around its neck. As soon as it was roped, the alligator began to swim back toward his home, which was a hole in the bank of the lake. He pulled Tobe across the lake in the boat at a dangerous speed in its wake.

The water was lower in the lake than usual because it had been so dry. The alligator had to go across a strip of land with no water over it; the boat lodged on the land. Tobe followed the gator to the mouth of his hole holding on to the rope. He took the rope and tied it to a button willow tree keeping all the slack out of it. He listened to and fought the gator all through the night, keeping out of its way.

When my dad and I located Tobe the next morning, he told us that he had the big alligator on the end of his rope. We looked the situation over and decided to get the truck around to that area so we could tie on to the rope and pull the alligator out. We found out that getting the alligator out of the water and into the truck was no easy task, as Tobe wanted him alive.

During the night, Tobe had gotten the alligator almost out of the hole. We were able to tie the rope to the pickup and after two or three tries, we got the gator to the top of the ground. The pickup could not pull him when he hooked his tail around any tree or palmetto. My dad would back up about three or four feet and gun the engine to jerk the gator loose. He would go several feet before the gator could get his tail around another tree and stop the truck.

We finally got him pulled into the truck. His tail was sticking out, so we had to fold it back. It took three of us to hold him down as we wired this mouth with bailing wire.

We kept him for a couple of months before he died. We think he died from pulling against the chains. People came from all over to see our big gator. We would pull him out with a chain. As we skinned him after he died, we found bullets from different size rifles and different size buck shot from a shot gun. Evidently people had shot him in the wild several times, and he had managed to survive those wounds. He just could not live with people pulling him around on a chain.

These early life experiences of the Harris lads were truly the beginning of the avocations to be followed by the brothers for years to come. They were to be at the draining of many lakes in the future in different parts of the wilderness from the West Fork of the San Jacinto to the far away Trinity. At each of those later draining's, Tobe was to be found using his wits to increase the alligator population in his lake at home. Later he learned to wrestle with them. He was to know them by their signs and the seasons of their changing temperaments.

Roy was to pursue his study of the primitive people who left their wondrous story written across the green earth. Piece by piece, through the years ahead, he was to assemble his artifacts and pieces of pottery to be placed in a case of a mat of cotton. He was destined to grow in knowledge of them until he could imagine the tribes living again on the hills overlooking the lakes.

In 1939, a third son, destined to become a Texas heavyweight golden gloves champion, was born to Henry and Gladys. They named him Henry. He was to grow up to be the strongest lad in Cut and Shoot. It was in "Little Henry's" third year that the clansmen had finally drained Carter's Lake. They flushed literally wagon loads of gar-fish from the muddy bottom. People from their humble homes in the forest who came down to the bank to watch the spectacle received rough fish as their rewards. Some of the buffalo fish weighed thirty pounds and upward. Of all the lakes the clansmen drained, the well of reptiles below the hill where Mateo had governed his people yielded the most bountiful harvest.

As the draining progressed, several of the men received bad gashes from gar-fish. Others had narrow escapes. Tobe and Roy stood on the bank and watched. Tobe could hardly restrain himself from answering the call of the wild urge to bog up to his ears in the mud and fasten his arms around the slipperiest and slimiest, and most dangerous thing he could find.

One of Tobe's favorite play grounds was a reptile-infested swamp on a rainy, lightening-filled night.

Left, Tobe Harris, Roy's brother, with their dad, Henry, and "friends"

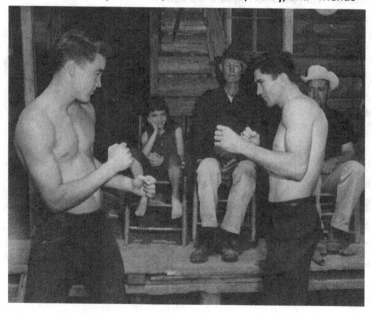

Backgroud, sitting, Roy's youngest sister, Patsy, Uncle Cleve and Roy's dad, Henry. Foreground: Left, Roy's brother, "Little" Henry, and Roy

Boxing ring by the Harris home, which boxing ring J.T. Montgomery procured from Madison Square Garden.

Roy's mother, Gladys; "Jim Dandy", Roy's youngest brother; and father, Henry

Sam Houston State's boxing team with coach, Glen Buffaloe, far right, standing. When Buffaloe was working at Conroe, at J. T. Montgomery's suggestion, he began to refer to his boxing team as from Cut and Shoot, thus launching the first big publicity blitz

Left to right, Uncle Cleve, Patsy and Little Henry.

Jack Dempsey, arguably the greatest heavyweight of all time, raises Roy's hand.

Roy Harris, shadow boxing

Roy gets in a good punch on an unidentified opponent.

Standing, "Big" Henry, while Roy's manager at the time, Benny King, ties Roy's gloves

Roy's brother, Tobe, admires the record-setting alligator which he caught, with a rope and a boat. The pond and gator are in the Harris front yard.

Roy on duty at Fort Sill, Oklahoma, shortly before the Patterson fight.

Professor Roy Harris admires his class.

Roy poses before memorabilia.

Roy spars with his brother, Henry

Roy with wife, Jean, surrounded by their six children: left to right, Rhonda, Robert, Connie, Keven and Sabrina. The youngest, in front, is Resa.

Young Roy, proud of an early trophy

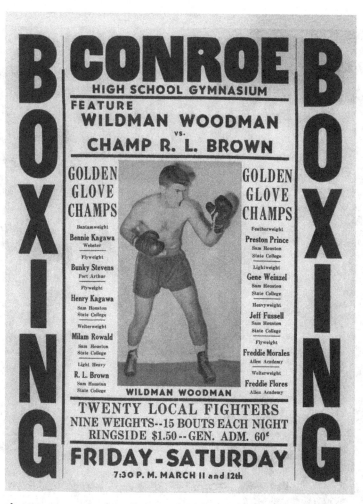

Boxing tournament advertisement in the early days: It features Campbell "Wildman" Woodman. Billed as the "Pride of Montgomery County", Wildman was the forerunner of the Cut and Shoot Boxing Dynasty. Note the "charming" ticket fees.

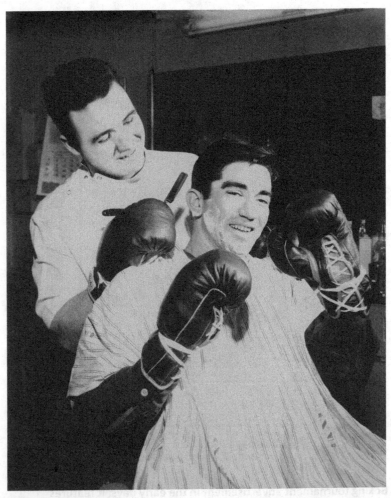

Publicity stunt for one of Roy's fights. His impending opponent gives him a "close shave."

Roy's dad, Henry, ready not to be messed with.

Back row, left to right are Roy's brothers, Little Henry and "Jim Dandy" and sisters, Francis and Wynne. Front, Roy, right, with "Coon" Massey, one of the clan's oldest and greatest friends.

Roy and his dad share a light moment.

Roy's wife, Jean, and friends. At far right is Joy Montgomery, wife of J.T. Montgomery and mother of co-author, Robin Montgomery.

A classic: Molders of the Cut and Shoot legend gather around the old and rugged ring in the front yard. Left to right, Roy, J.T. Montgomery, Big Henry, Tobe, Armadillo and Glen Buffaloe.

Chapter VII

THE SWAMP THING

Entering his junior high years, Roy would follow the woodsmen across the ancient battle grounds of the Orquoquisac, scratching redbugs and clawing at seed ticks in the daytime and slapping mosquitoes that whined through the camp smoke in the evening. His job was to hold unmarked pigs while the sharp knives of Bob and Big Henry whacked the proper identification marks in their ears. Tobe was the dabber. His job was to administer the antiseptic of turpentine and tar so that the blue flies wouldn't blow the cuts with screw worm eggs.

In between times, they hunted. Roe was getting old, but he came into camp one night in July with bloody claw-marks on his left hand. He mumbled while Henry doctored it, "There were a bear over there where we marked those speckled hogs in the Peach Creek country between here and Boggy. We was in there 'bout where Boggy runs into Peach Creek, an' I saw his tracks goin' into a bay gall that got knolls all out in 'em and ol' sweet bays growed all over 'em.

"That big track went into that bay gall a couple o' hours before sundown. I came back and got my winchester where I had it up to camp, to kill him. I knew he would eat me up if I went in there and missed near 'nough to wound him.

"He was a pretty good-sized bear. The dogs tracked him right up the trail. I had three dogs with me. You couldn't kick them yeller hounds when they smelled that bear track 'cause they were so close right 'neath your feet you couldn't kick em. It's the worse I ever saw a dog do.

"I took my winchester to target, an' I killed me four nice squirrels going up Peach Creek and decided I'd come up Boggy and kill a few more. I had that good squirrel dog of your'n, Henry, Ol' Ben. He was with me. He was doin' the treein' of the squirrels, and I had these two or three other dogs—I don't know how many. They'd help tree when Ben treed. He was a good squirrel dog, but he had to do all the work."

Roy and Tobe, especially Tobe, listened intently while Roe talked and Henry doctored his hand with boiled swamp water and turpentine.

"So I walked out in a trail," Roe continued, "and those dogs was back 'ahind me huntin', and I saw this track goin' up a cow trail just this side o' Boggy, and there was a heap o' blackberry vines just thick as straw as in a sweepin' broom through there. You get in those black berry patches at night. . . it was dark by the time I got in 'em . . . you couldn't hardly see your way out.

"I saw this track about there in the mud, an' it looked like a Indian track, cause it was barefooted. White man couldn't take the strain on his feet, with all the briars and stuff. I said, 'Good honk from a big goose, what's a Indian doin' over in these woods? He must have run off from where he belonged because of sumpthin' or 'nuther.

"I tracked him a little piece, an' as soon as I tracked him a little piece, I see it was a bear's track; I'd seen lots of 'em, I said. 'Uh, Oh! That's a track of a bear what's been berry pickin.'

"Just about the time I discovered it was a bear's track, those dogs run upon me, and they smelled him. He must a'v been just not too far ahead of me when I went along there, because they could smell it good, and boy, they commenced whinin' and about to howl, and they just run under my feet and bristled up; and Henry, I couldn't walk for 'em, and they never treed nary nuther squirrel. I went up to where he went into the bay gall and they never got two feet from me. They all tried to get under my feet.

"I left and went down the road, and they never got away from me 'til they got in a hunnerd 'n fifty yards of Peach Creek.

"I tracked that bear from way up Boggy an' I tell you, Henry, I traveled after dark, by moonlight in that swamp and I stepped from one knoll to another where some ol' roots and a little dirt is. When you step in between 'em you go up to your neck in dirty water. I bet Bob has fallen in a hunnerd, but he's not as old as me."

Henry interrupted Roe to tell him to get his story straight. He reminded him that he had said that he first saw a bear track and then went to camp for the gun. Afterwards, according to his story, he had leisurely hunted squirrels on his way back to the bay gall to kill the bear.

"Why in tarnation did you all of a sudden-like, find those bear tracks when you got back down there to Boggy like you hadn't seen 'em before?" Henry snorted. "I think you said you found 'em before you came after the gun!"

Roe saw that his story was mixed up so he tried to scratch his head with his lacerated hand, but Henry held it. The arrested movement let loose a stabbing pain in his hand and arm. He groaned a little then continued.

"Those bear swamps are hard as brushfire to get across if you don't know what you are a doin'. They're just little bumps around the trees like cypress knees, roots, and things. You can step from one to another and walk, but if you miss it, that between it don't have any bottom.

"I know you've been in all kinds of swamps, Henry, but you have never been in this one."

Trying to cut to the chase, Henry demanded, "Where's this bear? If it is a bear...or is it a bare-footed Indian out there?"

By now, Roe had convinced himself that what he saw were bear tracks.

"Henry," he insisted, "the bare-foot tracks I saw, prob'ly weren't Indian. They was prob'ly for sure, bear tracks."

"Well, that really clears it up, Roe," Henry blurted, sardonically.

Ignoring Henry's skepticism, Roe continued.

"I followed him out in the bay gall and got out there and missed my footin' and stepped off in that thing clear up to my neck. That's one of the times I made myself cuss, 'cause I was mussed up and I knew the bear was gettin' plum' away. Missed my footin' 'cause I was in such amount of hurry. Otherwise, would a' been no need to cuss."

Giving up temporarily on getting a straight answer, Henry tried another route. "How'd you get your hand clawed? Did the bear do it?" Henry asked, puzzled.

"Snappin' turtle done it," answered Roe. "He was a sittin' in some clump grass. I grabbed on to him when I came up for air after I fell in that bear wallow."

Cleve Murray, Henry's long lanky uncle-in-law, took a big dip of snuff, and as he began to talk, a spray of the stuff blew out of his mouth into Roe's turpentine soaked hand.

"Roe," Cleve drawled, while tonguing the snuff into a pocket formed by his lower lip, "you really reckon you saw a bear track?"

Roe rose up to his full height in righteous wrath. "Shore, I was there lookin' at 'um! What do you think perhaps I saw? Guess you think it was a parable, or miracle, or I was drunk?"

Cleve had his snuff well down in the puckered pocket of his lip by now, and his words came out much clearer.

"Tobe done led Roy off down to the bay gall," Cleve said, "to look for the bear while you got everybody mixed up with your consarned ramblin' around with your mouth, tryin' to get your story straight."

Henry gripped Roe by the wrist, just above his sore hand. "Roe, did you see those bear tracks or were you just making up a story? Tell me the honest truth," Henry blazed and demanded an answer. "My boys are out there!"

When Roe assured him that a big black bear really lurked in the swamp, Henry called his kinsmen to him with three short blasts of his hunting horn. He briefly told them of Roe's bear story and of Cleve's suspicion that Tobe and Roy had slipped out of camp to hunt down the bear.

Immediate preparations were made to follow the boys. It didn't take long to make them. Most of the dogs had to be tied up so they wouldn't go out into the night on a deer's trail, or otherwise disturb the business at hand with their different bayings at 'coons or 'possums. The only other thing to slow their departure was the few seconds spent on bridling the ponies.

Henry led the way. A dozen Walker dogs and a few black and tan hounds raced silently through the sweet gum thickets beside them, waiting to be shown tracks they were to follow.

Roe and Cleve, being rather ancient, and tired too, didn't join the hunt for the bear-hunting boys. They also remained in camp for another reason. Henry didn't want them along to be in the way any more than he wanted the tied-up dogs along.

Tired and turtle-torn as he was, Roe would have liked to have gone along, but since he couldn't, he sat on a cottonwood log and fretted.

Cleve fussed a little about the tied-up dogs howling their displeasure at not being with the others on the hunt, then took on a cheery grin as he recalled another anecdote about the merry men of the greenwood.

"Tobe laughed so much at Armadillo 'cause Susie broke off hers and Armadillo's romance," Cleve began, "that Armadillo took his long-tom single-barrel shotgun over to the woods in 'ahind Susie's house. He had egg-shaped fishing sinkers made out of lead with a hole through them to thread the fishin' line through. He took the bullets out of the shotgun shell and tramped in one of them sinkers. He called that kind of gun-load a 'blue whistler' 'cause the wind whistled through the center hole when it shot.

"Armadillo lay in amongst a bush heap 'til Susie came out of the house to go to the smoke house 'ahind the house. He gave her time to get busy at what she was doin' ' afore he pulled the trigger on the blue whistler. He shot over high so the whistler would screech into the shingles and make a powerful racket. I hear tell that Susie didn't pay no 'tention at that time to what happened, so that night, Armadillo pilfered some oil field alum and put a bucketful in her cistern. Susie went around all week with her lips all puckered up and Armadillo would ask her if she was puckered up to kiss him."

Roe fondled his torn hand to feel if it was hurt, but the turpentine had taken all the soreness out. He laughingly thought about Armadillo and the alum and forgot about his hand. He would rather talk about the folklore of the forest people than complain about his own miseries, anyhow.

"I come by Henry's one time when Tobe and Roy was little bitsy boys," Roe began. "I took them up town with me on a bale of cotton I hauled to the gin for a widow woman livin' up close to the school house."

Cleve looked sideways at Roe at the mention of the widow, but Roe paid no attention to his accusing expression.

"Tobe and Roy wanted to go to town with me," he continued. "I had a bale of cotton with the big hosses pullin' it, and I takes them with me to the gin.

"Well, I ginned the cotton, and the boys were messin' around there, and there was two little boomer kids there bigger'n Tobe and Roy. I don't know what the fracas come up about, but they got into a gosh awful squabble out there 'ahind the seed house. I had a seed fork. I think I was loadin' my seed, or unloadin' it. I don't know which I was doin', and Tobe and the little boomers was fightin'. They was holdin' him a pretty good battle, and Roy was tryin ' to hold first one and then the other off Tobe.

"There was some bolts" Roe was wound up in his story, "layin' there 'bout the size of sling-shot rocks. So I says to Tobe and Roy, "Why don't you pick up some of the bolts and bust them boomers?" Tobe got a bolt and knocked fire from the boomer kids. Then the old boomer come out and took sides with his kids.

"Tobe and Roy didn't know how to take on a whole big boomer in that day, but I just happened around in time with a seed fork, and I told that smart fellow to get from here or I'll stick this seed fork through his paunch. I was fixin' to do it and that boomer went, and the little ones went right behind him. Roy hasn't hit nobody yet. All he did was to try to pull them off Tobe. He hasn't said nothin' neither.

"That was quite a day," sighed Roe. "When we was comin' back to Cut and Shoot, there was a gypsy fortune teller outfit there on the hill at Butlersburg. Just as we turned the curve, there was their camp.

"A gypsy woman run out and tried to stop us," Roe told Cleve as though Cleve hadn't heard the story a dozen times before. 'It looked like it was goin' ta rain, and I had a ginned bale of cotton and some seed on the wagon, and I had to get home."

The two old friends and relatives could hear the Walker dogs picking up the bear's trail at the mouth of the bay gall, but Roe was wound up in his story. Cleve was listening to the deep-sounding voices of the dogs and the cow horn blasts filling the night with music. Roe thought he was listening to him.

"The gypsy woman run right out and tried to stop my hosses and I told her to get out of the way, but she run right up beside me and commenced to ask me to let her tell my fortune so she could get some money to buy some sugar for a sick woman. I knowed she was tellin' a yarn, so I told her to get out of the way so I could move on. But she kept hollerin' at us.

"I finally told her that I would give her some sugar for a sick woman. I took a big black snake whip out, and I was a good man then, and I blasted her all up and down that road. That whip was a poppin' like a forty-five and that woman was a hollerin' and yellin' and she took a run through the woods.

"I yelled at her and told her, "I'll give you money for a sick woman!" Tobe was just sittin' up in the wagon a lookin' and learnin' how to be mean. Roy looked sick around his face when the whip was a poppin' until he saw the gypsy wasn't no woman a 'tall when she run through the weed patch. Roy saw them men's clothes on underneath the dress. He sat on the cotton bale and grinned when the gypsy woman cussed like a man what she was. Tobe didn't take kindly to the cussin'. He jumped off the wagon and picked up a handy club and knocked the imposter down in the weed patch.

With a sigh and a deep breath, Cleve rinsed his mouth out with some of the left-over coffee from one of the woodsmen's cups.

"Wanna swig?" he asked Roe. "It sure do make a body feel better for another dip.

Roe walked stiffly away from the fire in the direction of the keg, but his rheumatism wouldn't permit him to hurry. Too, his mangled hand was stiffening in the night air.

" 'Hope Tobe and Roy don't run upon that alligator terrapin," he sighed as he held his hand. "His ol' snout is short and pointed above his chin wattles, an' he looks at you narrow between the eyes."

Tobe and Roy were having their troubles in the boggy swamp, as darkness had fallen. Long before they heard the woodsmen's horn, they had gone, by lighter-kindling light, several hundred yards across the swamp's surface by pulling themselves through an amazing network of naked roots. Those roots spread-eagled from their tree trunks about a foot above the water line and flared in serpentine rainbows downward to the muddy bottom.

Tobe found pleasure in watching the enormous amphibia slithering beneath his feet through the eerie water labyrinth. He reveled in the sodden drama that unfolded itself in successive stages as the torch light dispelled the curtain of darkness now hanging heavily over the forgotten prehistoric bog.

Roy shook his head. Doubtless he was enjoying himself, but to save his life he couldn't reason why. It would be later in his college biology classes that he would delve into the mysteries of hereditary behavior in humans. It would suffice for tonight that he take things for granted and follow his brother toward who knows what adventure awaited them. Hairy branches of slender swamp privet provided holds for the boys. When they often times slipped on the slimy tree knees, the forestiera limbs would be shaken, resulting in purple shadows of privet fruit cascading into the water. The pelting sounds of the one-seeded stones alarmed a myriad of creatures. The innocuous hellbender hung by his yellow toes to the silver bell bushes, surveying the swamp for a polliwog supper. Tobe called them mudpuppies. He had caught those twenty-inch salamanders lots of times on worm-baited hooks.

Roy loved to study the vegetation of the wild wood.

The woods in our area had many different kinds of trees: probably 20 kinds of oak, chinquapin, hickory nut, may haw, sweet gum and black gum, magnolia, elm, red haw, huckleberry (which we used as food for animals), sycamore, pine, prickly ash, black walnut, button willow, Chinaberry, mulberry and Spanish mulberry. Grapes and muscadines grew wild and plentiful. Cypress trees grew in the low areas. Some cacti grew along with ironwood trees. Many pecan trees grew in the bottom land. Another nut, called the pignut, grew and had nuts like hickory nuts but was bitter; the squirrels and hogs loved them. A lot of trees produced food for animals as well as for people. Another interesting item: Spanish mulberry made the best toilet paper in the woods. Living in the country as we did, very little that nature provided us went to waste.

There in the swamp, something stayed the brothers-errant for an instant, taking their minds off a study of the trees and plants. As the weather turned, a forked flash from the heavens had paled their torchlight into insignificance. At the same time a growling sound emitted from a nearby coral bean thicket. In Texas a coral bean bush is also called bear berry.

The sound reverberated through the still night air until it reached a crescendo of uncanny echoes among the cypress trees. The fiendish wailing took on a diabolical significance when a second splintering blaze from the firmament revealed the swamp in the ghostly reality of its ugliness. A semitropical deluge was in the offing while a wild demented creature was screaming from the coral beans either at the Harris boys or because the approaching storm upset the barometric electrodes of his nerve ends.

Tobe gave Roy a foot-lift up a black gum tree. "Climb up to the top, Roy, an' see what's out there. I expect we've lucked ourselves into a mess of fun."

On cue, Roy frog-kicked his way up the furrowed bark of the tree until he reached its mid-level branches. As he paused to survey the scene, the eastern sky lit up his scouting countenance with electrical light. He gazed into its grandeur with the same serene composure he was in later years to fasten upon the flicking jabs of Willie Pastrano, the world light-heavyweight champion.

Out there in the wastelands a tortured beast was bellowing. Roy shook himself like a coffee bean weed in a whirlwind as his studious eyes swept all below him, but he hated the awful wail that continued to shatter its stillness. While long lightning streaks zigzagged their multimillion volts across the boiling cumulonimbus, he wrapped his left elbow around a stable limb of the tree. Secure in his perch, he felt his pocket to be sure his knife, with its ever-sharp blade, was there, ready for just such an occasion. As he watched, a faint quarter moon hung its lower hook into the rushing storm.

Soon he became aware that in the treetop above him appeared to be a despondent panther complaining to the swampy, insect ridden world that his woes were paramount. Maybe, so the boy thought, for that reason the feline was trying to out-lung the faint peals of thunder that now and then were audible. Maybe it was because his stomach was empty or perhaps, Roy surmised, one of the opposite sex might have spurned the squalling beast. Whatever the reason might be, Roy felt the best defense was to keep calm, even as he continued to be ready at an instance's notice to retrieve his knife. If his suspicions were correct, the brute would be sorely vexed at his presence and a sharp blade could come in mighty handy.

Meanwhile, Tobe had crawled a ways up the tree below Roy where greeting him were racy streaks of fire visible through the tree tops. Blustering thunderheads began to divide the earth and sky, prying the prime exponents of creation apart to give a premature birth to the creatures of the swamp. As if awakening to life, the primordial fastness suddenly came alive with a myriad of noises. Katydids and crickets vied with multitudes of tree frogs to command the soprano section of the swampy symphony. A great horned owl hooted and chatted to his fussy cousins as he sailed like a specter through the droopy moss-covered foliage.

The red-headed Tobe rested on his perch on the black gum tree looking the counterpart of his grandfather. He was mud-besmeared as though he had slept beneath a clay root. A cap that had once been the outer adornment of a sow coon was held in his hand while he wiped the sweat from his forehead with his dirty right hand. Below him drifted the screams of some unknown species, mingled with splashes of alligator gars in the hyacinth-locked mire between them. The coming storm was breaking the creepy stillness and a thousand thicket noises suddenly trebled on the wind with the panther's shrieks.

"That thing sure sounds like a lost woman," Tobe observed as Roy continued at the ready for what he suspected would soon be a battle with a furry beast.

"Sounds like one, alright," concurred Roy. "And I believe she is right above us."

The driving rain pelted their upturned faces as they surveyed the branches, by lightning light, for the swamp thing that was uttering those frightful screams. To get a better focus, both boys began to ascend higher up the tree.

Reaching some ten feet above the swamp, they suddenly stopped climbing. There! The panther indeed occupied the branches just above their heads. But, it was not looking at the two boys. Instead, it focused its tortured gaze on something stirring in the marshy waters below where a churning, squirming figure languished in the mud.

As yet another flash of lightening sped through the swamp, the boys saw that the figure below was human . . . And, witnessing the figure struggling to secure its footing it became clear that it was bare-footed!

"Roe was right the first time," Tobe said. "He really did see tracks of a bare-footed man, not a bear.

"But," Tobe's face began to take on a sinister grin. "That's no Indian."

"Well, what is it?" Roy inquired, anxious for Tobe's revelation.

"You won't believe this, Roy. That is Armadillo!"

"Good grief," snapped Roy. "What in tarnation could he be doin' out here . . . and bare-footed . . . in this ole swamp?"

Recognizing the boys, and seeing them immersed in, to him, casual conversation, Armadillo cried, "Will you two buzzards hush and help me catch that blasted cat what's a growlin' right above you?"

"What 'a you want to do with him?" Tobe asked, now surprisingly calm in spite of the fact that a crazed and huge feline lurked just above him.

"I want to take him home to scare Susie," a very wobbly and abstracted Armadillo said.

"Look's as how Armadillo's so flustered over his girlfriend that he doesn't know what he's about tonight," observed Tobe to Roy.

"Yes, I heard she's been givin' him a real hard time lately and he's crazy in pain right now, wonderin' around, not knowin' what he's doin'", agreed Roy.

Suddenly, the boy's pondering reached an abrupt halt as the great beast leaped downward. With his descent, the cat leaped so closely that rancid feline breath enveloped the faces of the Harris boys. The cat was on a path, a la a dive bomber, right at Armadillo.

At that moment, the scene grew dark; the boys could discern nothing below. The only sounds were of erratic rustlings in the muddy mire, interspersed with growls of the panther.

"Oh my," Tobe cried, "The panther attacked Armadillo."

Instantly, both the boys jumped aiming to land on the feline, quickly to retrieve their knives and engage the beast in furious battle. Even as they were in the air, however, the panther ran away, dragging his prey with him in those huge jaws.

Upon landing in the murky swamp floor, Tobe and Roy struggled to their feet seeking to chase the panther, only to stumble over a creature arising from the deep mud.

It was their very unsteady friend, Armadillo.

Rubbing the mud from his eyes, Armadillo mumbled, "'hope ol' pant'er enjoys that little shoat of a hog he just lit onto."

Chapter VIII

REMINISCENCES:

Roy's formative years in the ring

Roy finished the ninth grade of the Conroe Junior High School in May, 1948 with an overall achievement average of ninety-three. This was not such an amazing accomplishment when his intelligence quotient of one hundred and thirty-two is taken into account. It was good enough, however, to rank him third in his graduation class of one hundred and fifty-six.

His years in that school had been full to overflowing. A primary influence was Mrs. Maude Bell. When Roy was in the seventh grade she was his homeroom teacher. Years before she taught his mother. She indoctrinated his fertile brain with the pure philosophy in which all reason and logic are wrapped, sending him into his other classes in a deliberate mood to accept the things his teachers knew about the wisdom of the ages.

In her younger years, Mrs. Bell had driven each morning in a buggy from her humble home in Conroe, down eight muddy miles to the very humble school at Dry Creek. She knew the people in the sylvan shades of Cut and Shoot. They loved her for her industry. They loved her for her sincerity. Most of all they loved her because she was plain and lovable Mrs. Bell.

Through those formative days of puberty and early adolescence Roy studied boxing in his physical education classes. Each boy in school was required to learn the basic techniques of the sport and to take special calisthenics to train his body to respond to the eventualities that would later confront him in the ring.

The theory behind it was that a boy at that particular age was pliable enough to absorb any kind of arm-delivered blows from a lad of similar age in the same weight. Punching power was not yet prevalent in their make-up, but hero-worship was. Boys of that age group liked stories about Beowulf, The Brave Prince; Siegfried, The Useful Warrior; and Roland, The Noble Knight. They also read about Tarzan. In Sunday school and in their intermediate classes, they learned to love Samson and David and other Biblical heroes.

Roy learned, together with his classmates, that no sport could be mastered until the brain was trained to envelope its entire philosophy. The studious Roy had no trouble comprehending this concept, neither did he linger long mulling over a simple fact, repeated over and over to his class, that next to the brain in any kind of locomotive sport was flawless footwork.

He learned that his arms were next, then the body, driven by a stout heart pumping streams of fresh red blood over his entire being. Following that easy little pattern of physical training, scores of boys became adept at the art of self-defense—Wildman Woodman, Chester Lee, "Caveman" Bradley, Don Granger, Ringo, Johnny and Buddy Hopkins, Billy Giles and many, many others who fought visiting Golden Gloves Champions in the Conroe Tournaments, and won. Each year the Cut and Shoot lads led the way because they had the same teaching at home that they received in school. They received it in school because their physical education teacher had learned it from Henry Harris.

That physical education teacher was J.T. Montgomery. Roy addresses this period of his life and discussed several of the boxers with whom he trained in that day.

When I went to Junior High School, we had a principal by the name of J.T. Montgomery, and he loved boxing. He had started boxing in the Junior High School in Conroe for the male students in the boxing class at school. Mr. Montgomery, as a boxing coach before he became a principal, weighed all of his boys in physical education, and we were placed into weight divisions in brackets of 10 pound differences . . .110-120, 120-130, etc. Everyone who weighed over 175 was in the same weight bracket which was heavyweight. I weighed 86 pounds.

Roy tells an interesting story during these times about how events maneuvered him into a public match with his brother, Tobe:

There were several boys in each weight bracket, including my brother, Tobe. In one tournament in the semi-finals, in my bracket, I fought a boy that was really tough and gave him a hard battle, but I burst his mouth and nose and blackened his eyes. When he went home, his mother withdrew him from the boxing and would not allow him to fight my brother, Tobe, in the finals.

Another good fighter in our weight who had been beaten in the bracket that Tobe was in was put back into my bracket so he could fight Tobe in the final after he beat me. I beat him by a TKO, and then he quit. This put me in the finals where I was scheduled to fight Tobe. We had a good fight, about what we did every evening at home, and I won the decision in the fight.

I received a certificate for boxing in the Travis Junior High Boxing Tournament (which was my first claim to fame in boxing) when I was in the 7th grade and was 13 years old. Mr. Montgomery continued to promote boxing in the area, and I was able to fight in most of the tournaments that took place in the Conroe area. Mr. Montgomery brought in other schools from other towns to fight our Conroe boxers.

Roy tells the story of how, during these early years, a world famous boxing ring came to Conroe Jr. High, then later made its way to the Harris home grounds at Cut and Shoot:

Mr. Montgomery did not know where to find a boxing ring to hold the events for the school. The boxing classes in Junior high were held in the gymnasium with lines drawn to represent the ring, and the punching bags were located in the dressing room of the gym. He wanted something better for the boys. He contacted the Boxing Commission in New York to find out where he could purchase a real boxing ring. The old rings consisted of three ropes, and the new rings required four ropes to keep boxers from falling through to the floor.

The old ring used by the promoter who promoted the fight between Joe Louis and Max Smelling, the German heavyweight champion, was available for purchase. Mr. Montgomery made a deal with those people and purchased the old ring for approximately $400.00 and had it shipped to Travis Junior High in Conroe. The ring was consequently owned by the Conroe Independent School District for several years, but after boxing was no longer offered at Travis, the ring was no longer needed. The ring lay in storage for several years before the school district wanted to sell the ring to get it out of storage and out of the way. Mr. Montgomery called me and asked if I wanted to buy the ring. I told him that I did, and I purchased it from the school district.

I built a building to house the new boxing ring. Young boxers continued showing up and working out in the evenings with us, and this gave us a much better place to work out than the old ring under the gas flare. The building had electric lights, and the ring had good padding under a good canvas cover. I was in college at the time I bought and moved the ring in 1957 and was now boxing professionally. This is the same ring that I had used to prepare for several fights in preparation for my world title bout against Floyd Patterson.

Most of the Conroe boys that fought in the tournaments worked out at the Harris boxing gym in Cut and Shoot. Our Conroe boxers were fighting boxing teams from Houston and other cities around our area. Mr. Montgomery was responsible for getting a lot of our young boys in the area to learn how to box well enough to become regional and state champions in the

Golden Gloves, the Olympics and other boxing events. Wildman Woodman, Don Granger, Fred Rice, Darrell Brumley, Wayne (Killer) Vaughn and his brothers, Clarence and Perry, Johnny Hopkins and brother, Buddy Hopkins, Tobe, Henry Harris (my younger brother) and I were examples of those he helped.

Mr. Montgomery continued working with us in Junior High in the boxing club throughout my junior high days. He also continued visiting our boxing gym at home and along with Emmett Houser, attended my world championship bout against Floyd Patterson in California in 1958. Mr. Montgomery was a very strong, positive influence in my life and career. He, my dad, and Glen Buffaloe, were all good coaches.

Wildman Woodman, already referred to several times in these pages—remember the christening of the name Victor by Henry Harris?-- was the forerunner of the fighting Cut and Shooters. Trained by both J. T. Montgomery and Henry Harris, he was special in many ways, a singer, could play both the acoustic and the steel guitar, and was good in other sports, especially football in which sport he later won a college scholarship.

Campbell Victor (Wildman) Woodman is a good example of one of the earlier fighters my dad trained. Wildman was one of the best fighters in the nation in his earlier boxing days, although he was a very small child at the time of his birth. One of the ladies at his birth commented that he was such a "tiny boy". This name stuck with him, and he was often called Tiny Boy as well as Wildman. He did not remain small, as he fought in his boxing career as a light heavyweight.

Wildman won the state golden gloves championship. He had a real good knockout punch with his right hand and a good left jab. Wildman was good with little tricks that would help him to win battles in the ring. For instance, he would lower his left hook over the right hand. He would lower his right hand to invite the opponent to jab his face. Woodman would lean backwards with the jab and follow it back in with the right hand over the jab.

This was a very hard punch, and Wildman knocked out lots of fighters with this trick. He was a guitar picker and a singer along with being a boxer. He was a popular announcer on the radio in Conroe. He went to college on a football scholarship to Midwestern in Wichita Falls, Texas. He continued to fight while in college and even after he became a teacher/coach.

Roy tells a special story about Wildman and his horse:

Wildman Woodman had a horse named Old Dan Patch that he rode from his home to our place, which was about three miles. Evidently Tiny Boy, as we called him, had spent many hours working with the horse that was named for a famous racehorse. One day while he was at our house, he left Old Dan Patch standing out in the yard by the house with his saddle and bridle still on him. Old Dan was grazing. Wildman said, "Old Dan is getting old. He looks sick like he doesn't feel good."

Dan lowered his ears and his head and looked like he was really sick and feeling bad. Wildman would say, "Old Dan is really sick. I think he is going to die." Dan would droop like he was going to fall down and then lay down. While he was down, Wildman would say, "I think he is going to die." Dan would roll on his side. Wildman would comment that Dan was dead. Dan would suck in air to bloat his stomach and look like he had been dead for a day or two. He would remain in that position until Tiny Boy would say, "I believe that Dan is getting better, it looks like he is going to be okay." Dan would roll over and get up.

We learned from this incident that many times animals hear and understand what we are saying, and they respond to what they hear. We all enjoyed watching and seeing Tiny Boy and Old Dan Patch perform.

(Parenthetically, Wildman and Robin Montgomery, co-author of this work, once had a band called "Robin and the Wild Robineers" that had a regular spot on Saturday afternoons on Conroe's first radio station, KMCO. Also in the band was a later brother-in-law of

Roy's, Edwin Rice, and Buddy Moorhead, for whom the Conroe football stadium was later named)

Roy makes special mention in his memoirs about another boxer from the Cut and Shoot area, a good friend of Wildman and also an exceptional football player like Wildman. He also played college football. This was Don Granger.

Don Granger was another boxer who trained with us. He was a good fighter who was very religious. He refused to talk ugly or use trash as others did. The worst thing I ever heard him say was "chicken headed rascal." There was one time when he had put an anvil over his head which weighed about 150 pounds. He was 17 or 18 years of age at the time and was so proud of this accomplishment, and he wanted Big Henry [Roy's dad] to see him. I saw him when he put the anvil up, but when my dad came to watch him, he could not get it up again. His feelings were hurt and that is when he said those famous bad words.

In one of the Conroe tournaments, Don was in the feature fight of the night against George Ringo, who was a good athlete and a famous Conroe High School football player. Don lost on a split decision to Ringo. Don was also an outstanding football player at Conroe High School and received a scholarship to Midwestern in Wichita Falls. Granger coached and taught in the

Conroe School System for several years before taking over the family business in Grangerland.

Armadillo also boxed in Jr. High for Mr. Montgomery. Roy has a memorable anecdote about Armadillo's experience in the ring:

"When Armadillo was in junior high in the boxing program, he was scheduled to fight another boxer at the school tournament. He did not have a mouth piece to wear when his bout was ready to start. Armadillo did not have any teeth left in his mouth, so Mr. Montgomery gave him a piece of cotton to help protect his gums saying that he did not need a mouth piece. Taking the cotton out of his mouth and washing it between rounds was quite a sight. We were so busy watching the cotton washing that we did not pay much attention to the real fight that ended in a draw.

Roy developed good habits and developed lasting friendships among his boxing buddies as his amateur career advanced. But he was ever studious, a true student of the boxing game. Let him tell the story:

Boxing has been one of the best things that ever happened to me. I still don't understand how a fighter from the backwoods of Cut and Shoot managed to do as well as I did in the field of boxing where so many great boxers were striving to do the same.

I know I had some talent, but so did others. I had a quick right hand, but so did others. I think I achieved where many others failed because my dad spent so much time training me, and he believed in me and made me believe in myself. And, I was unbelievably determined. I strove to do the best I could at whatever I was attempting to do at any time, whatever it might take.

I knew that in order for me to do better than anyone else, I had to try and push myself to the limit. I would outwork anyone. If someone asked me if I could walk on my hands, I would try. Then I would keep trying until I could do it. That is how I faced life. I could stand on my hands leaning against the wall and do pushups. I would let my head down to touch the floor and then push myself back up, keeping my body straight and then repeat the procedure as many times as I desired. I practiced until I could do the pushups perfectly. This made my arms stronger. I always drank fresh milk which helped develop my bones. I learned to stand on one foot, squat down and touch my rear to my heels and get back up without using my other foot or hand. It was a strength and balance project that helped me have good balance as well as strength in my legs. Once again, I practiced until it was perfect. Determination ruled my life.

Once I decided to become a boxer, I wanted to be the best I could. I wanted to learn how others did it so

I could do it better than they did. Actually, I wanted to learn how to fight to protect myself. I do not like to be hit! Nearly every athlete or boxer had a certain way of doing things that made him outstanding in his field of endeavor, whatever it was. Some methods worked well and others did not. I felt like I had to try different methods until I found one that worked for me. Most boxers that I came in contact with had a certain ability that made them good enough to be a competitor.

These qualities that made them better than the ordinary boxer allowed me to learn how to avoid their principal ability while boxing them. If a fighter had a good left hook or a good straight right or any other outstanding boxing ability that helped him to win his fights, I would train until I was able to avoid their primary weapon. I would work until I could neutralize their boxing ability, and they could not use these weapons against me. I tried to make them realize that their abilities on which they depended did not work on me. That discouraged them and made them easier for me to outbox and eventually win a decision over them.

Some fighters were outstanding, hardhitting punchers who depended on hitting their opponent and knocking him out. As far as boxing skills, they did not have many but they could get in and hit the opponent quickly and hard and knock him out. Other fighters may not hit hard enough to knock the opponent out, but had a tremendous amount of speed and accuracy with the punches. Those boxers were defensive fighters who threw a lot of punches and continually out boxed their opponents. They could beat an opponent so badly after one or two rounds of severe beatings, the opponent would give up and lose the bout.

I was a defensive boxer most of the time. Some of my opponents were real aggressive and depended on getting in close and knocking out the opponent. I liked to make them miss and counter punch them and try to take advantage of their inability to land their Sunday punch. With some of my opponents that were hard punchers with either hand and very aggressive in their boxing style, I would leave my corner quickly, rush to meet them in the center of the ring or even before they got out of their corner good, and hit them with a hard right hand. Most of the time I would be able to knock them out with a few blows. This was because they came into the ring expecting me to be a defensive fighter and give them the privilege of being the aggressor in the bout.

I always tried to enter a boxing match being well prepared for that fight. I tried to gather as much information as I could about my opponent and how he fought. I wanted to enter the fight prepared to go the full distance in full blast and come out as the winner at the end of the battle. I have seen so many fighters that were really good fighters but failed to get in good physical condition which caused them to lose a fight to someone that they could have whipped if they had properly prepared themselves for the physical battle.

Roy tells a story about a fighter friend of his who didn't live up to his potential.

There was a boxer I knew who did more training than he did actual boxing. He was fighting a boxer out of Houston, at a local bar that sponsored boxing matches in the Cut and Shoot area. The boxer from Houston was a hard puncher and had knocked out many other boxers. The fighter I knew had out boxed him for two rounds and almost all of the third and last round of the fight. There was probably less than 10 seconds before the end of the fight, and the other fighter hit [my friend] with a good hard right hand. My friend immediately stuck his hands out toward him and yelled, "Hold it. I know when I have had enough! The fight is over!" The referee raised the other fighter's hand as the winner. My friend could not have lost the fight if he had just done nothing and let the seconds expire, which they would have before the other fighter could have hit him again. He did not like to be hit!

Roy tells of another unusual incident concerning a fighter for whom Roy had great respect:

There are many funny and amusing incidents and happenings that come to mind concerning boxers. Once incident concerned Johnny White, a middleweight boxer to whom I had lost a decision in a fight at the college he was attending.

In the middleweight division of the State Golden Gloves in Fort Worth, there was a well-known military fighter who had the most outstanding fight record I had ever heard of. He had 249 amateur fights and had won 199 by knockouts. He was expected to whip Johnny White for his 250th fight and 200 wins by knockouts. This all sounds unreasonable to me, but he was a great amateur fighter and had knocked out everyone until he met Johnny White. Johnny knocked him out in the first round and surprised everyone except himself.

Johnny was one of the best boxers in the state. He had been fighting in the Golden Gloves for several years and was attending some college over in Northeast Texas. During the hunting season he was crawling through a fence with a loaded gun that misfired and shot him in one leg close to the hip. The leg had to be removed and this ended his boxing career.

Later when he was a salesman, he was driving a car and came up behind another car stopped for a red light. Johnny's wooden leg slipped off of the brake, and his car went forward and hit the car in front of him. The bump against the car in front of him was not hard enough to damage the car very much. The driver of the other car was a large and muscular, angry person who got out of his car and came back and started cussing at Johnny yelling at him that "If you get out of that car, I will beat some sense into you."

Johnny replied, "I had a better offer back up the road; a man offered to first pull me out of the car and then beat the heck out of me." This made the man even angrier. Johnny got out and the man swung at him, not knowing that Johnny was a boxer or that he was one-legged. Johnny hit the man with a good, straight right hand and knocked him out. Johnny drove off, but someone got his tag numbers from his license plates, and he was called to court.

When the judge called the case, Johnny began to walk toward the Judge's bench along with the angry man after the accident. Johnny had left the wooden leg at home and had folded his pants leg up to the hip and was using two crutches, limping badly as he walked. The judge, on his own, began to say, "The one thing that makes me madder than anything else is for a big, strong person to jump on and fight a cripple person." The bully immediately yelled, 'Judge, I am not Johnny White; he is the one who hit me.' The judge pounded the gavel and yelled, 'Get out of my court, and don't ever come back! I don't like to see a cripple man taken advantage of. Case dismissed!"

Roy's early years in the ring brought him fond memories and lasting friendships among fellow pugilists, preparing him well to make Cut and Shoot a name of renown.

Chapter IX

DEEP IN THE HEART OF TEXANS

Roy stood at the end of a table in his mother's kitchen idly fingering a patent medicine calendar that was hanging on the wall. It was New Year's Day, 1950. Finally, he took it down, but before he tossed it in the trash can, he said to his mother, "This has been a full year. I hope I learned some lessons that will stay with me through the nineteen fifties."

Those two sentences made a long speech for the quiet unassuming lad. Ordinarily he chose to listen and learn.

Indeed it had been a full year for him. He had won a boxing tournament in March. In April, during the Easter season, he had made up his mind to do the very best he could to prove to his kinsmen that he was truly one of them. In thinking back to those midnight hours on the San Jacinto River, the words of Roe about the crow and the chicken hawk still stuck in his mind. With those memories in mind he looked solemnly through an unscreened window to where a hedge of wild yellow jasmine was climbing up the barn. Long he looked, but he didn't see it. His thoughts were on the future.

""Reckon I'm gonna fight in the Golden Gloves this year, Gladys. What do you think about that?"

He didn't want to do anything to disturb his mother's peace of mind without first talking it over with her, even if the discussions were only brief and pointed.

"If that is what you want to do, son, it is all right with me."

She was as soft spoken as the son who favored her, and who was so much like her in so many ways. She didn't express herself in the idioms used by the backwoodsmen. In her school days at Trinity and later in Conroe, she had finished at the head of her class and it was from her and their father that her children learned the value of an academic education.

Their father taught them to search for the truth and not to believe something just because it was written in a book or a newspaper. "That book is wrong," he would say then give valid evidence to make his point. Regardless of his own beliefs, however, Henry encouraged his children to read and study books that they brought to the house. Then he would ask them to explain to him the things they had read, and many times he would prove to them that the author was wrong or, on the other hand, substantiate the validity of the text.

The point of Henry's approach was to teach his and Gladys's children the process of evaluation. "It's not best," he would say, "to swallow everything a book says for a fact. Most times you must use common horse sense,' cause you can't always carry books everywhere you go and hunt out answers to all the questions you're gonna face in this life."

Roy had been evaluating his training method. He had trained in a leisurely manner since the preceding Easter. Each morning and evening he had done the things he had determined to do that night nine months before while Hominy lay in a stupor on the hard ground after his companions with compassion, had retrieved him from the bay gall.

Roy had neglected nothing that he reasoned would help him to mold his body into the physical proportions toward which he had so methodically planned. But as far as boxing was concerned, he was still trying to solve that equation in the perennial yard-workouts with Tobe. He learned a lot from them but not nearly enough, he thought.

Roy, Tobe and several of their bearded kinsmen went to Lufkin, Texas for the regional Golden Gloves Tournament held on Friday and Saturday nights, January 27 and 28th, 1950. Tyson Payne, Sports Editor for the *Lufkin Daily News* wrote (later copied by the Conroe Courier February 2, 1950) in his column, "Payned Expressions":

> Lufkin fight fans opened wide their hearts during the Golden Gloves and enveloped Tobe and Roy Harris of [Cut and Shoot,] Texas.
>
> The two kids from the backwoods came up to Lufkin to make a good showing in the squared circle and that's just what they did. As this is written we do not know how the boys fared in their fighting Saturday night, but we know that whether they won or lost, Lufkin will not soon forget them.
>
> The youngsters, who were accompanied by their father and Uncle Bob, probably never saw such a crowd as was assembled in the gym Friday night, but they weren't left alone in their great adventure.
>
> The local fight fans hopped on their bandwagon right quick and no fighter on the card Friday night drew such applause and cheers as did the sunny-dispositioned youngsters from [Cut and Shoot.]
>
> The crowd whooped and hollered for several minutes after each Harris boy was declared winner.
>
> It was a heart-warming spectacle Friday night when the Harris boys were in the ring. It made one believe in the future of America, where the folks are always ready to pull for the underdog no matter where he is from and

where two boys from the deepest forest, who have had a minimum of education, can get in the same ring with college boys and meet them on their own terms. And where the boys meet and shake hands after the fight regardless of who the winner might be.

Communism will have to go a long way to match that kind of good old Americanism.

In his long column, Tyson Payne then recorded some of the reactions of the Cut and Shooters to their experience:

The trip to Lufkin was something new to Tobe and Roy, especially the part which saw them spend their first night in a hotel.

The two boys spent the night at the Angelina hotel, while their father and Uncle Bob had to head back to Conroe for the day, before returning to root for the boys in the Saturday night finals.

The boys found some strange things in the hotel and they were especially puzzled as to how they could find out the time by picking up the telephone and inquiring.

Uncle Bob had his perplexed moments, too. Friday night at the fight the public address announcer, Lee Friesen, asked him to stand up and take a bow.

Uncle Bob could hear his name being called but he couldn't find Friesen. He kept looking over in the corner towards the speaker, while Friesen was back in the other direction at the microphone.

Finally, Uncle Bob had to ask someone, "Say where is that fella anyway?"

He got up in the ring, took his bow and received a large ovation from the crowd.

Payne summarized the Cut and Shoot part of the Lufkin tournament in another article in the same paper under the dateline as follows:

Two boys from [Cut and Shoot], Texas, Tobe and Roy Harris, won the loudest applause from the over 500 fight fans who crowded into the Shands Gym Friday night to watch the opening night of the 1950 regional Golden Gloves Tournament. The cheers and applause were directed at the Harris boys from the backwoods . . .

The [Cut and Shoot] boys, together with their father, Henry and even more bearded Uncle Bob, put on a real show to the delight of the Lufkin fight fans.

****

In the third welter battle, Roy decisioned Tony Rusk of Sam Houston College, last year's middleweight champion. The [Cut and Shoot] lad, who had to give away three inches in height and three inches in reach to Rusk, had the crowd behind him 100 percent.

Harris had to jump off the floor to land blows to Rusk's face, but he did so often and with such effectiveness that the judges gave him a split decision.

****

In the light weight division, Tobe Harris won a unanimous decision over Charles Whatley of Sam Houston.

When the announcer raised Roy's hand that night in Lufkin, Cut and Shoot became an integral part of the commonwealth of Texas communities. The Lone Star State looked to its ledger to see if the place had been entered on its books. They found it to have been a Star Route in the nineteen twenties, radiating from Conroe, and they wondered how it received its name.

Reporters from the several great cities of Texas converged on Conroe. Their first question was about the Harris's. Their second concerned Cut and Shoot, and citizens of Conroe could answer neither of them. They were afraid in that day to venture too far into the Big Thicket country and to rub elbows with its bold inhabitants. A ring-side seat at the Conroe Boxing Tournament was as close as most of the citizens of Conroe had ever been to the children of the bearded forest giants. So the reporters turned to the school system to gather their information and to meet Tobe and Roy.

The principal, J.T. Montgomery, had suggested to the boxing coach whom he hired that the boxing team might take the name of Cut and Shoot to increase publicity for the program. The coach, Glen Buffaloe, took the suggestion and ran with it, launching a phenomenon.

Glen Buffaloe was hired by Mr. Montgomery at Travis Junior High to coach. He was helping train me and the Cut and Shoot boxing team before we went to Lufkin to fight in the Regional Golden Gloves Tournament in 1950. Glen was a former All Service Champion boxer in the Army and also was once a sparring partner for Joe Louis, former world heavyweight boxing champion. Buffaloe later became the boxing coach for Sam Houston State Teachers College. He helped Cut and Shoot get a lot of publicity for its boxing.

He went to the Conroe newspaper several times and asked them to write stories about our boxing, but they did not write any stories until he took our fighters to Lufkin to fight in the 1950 Regional Golden Gloves Tournament. He suggested that we fight from the city of Cut and Shoot rather than Conroe. The name caught on quickly and brought in publicity as well as national attention from newspapers all over the United States.

Tobe and I both won our weight in Lufkin and were then eligible to fight in the State Golden Gloves Tournament in Ft. Worth. Tobe was a welterweight, and I was a middleweight. Both of us were defeated in the state tournament. Glen did not stay long coaching in Conroe, but he did help me while he was there. I worked with him later after he began coaching at Sam Houston, and I was in high school.

Roy also writes his impressions of the Lufkin trip:

The Harris clan was such a spectacle that the people in downtown Lufkin would follow us around. About ten of us went into a restaurant and sat down when about 50 people crowded around outside at the windows of the restaurant looking in to see what we were doing. There were so many people outside that other folks had a hard time getting down the sidewalk or going in or out of the restaurant.

One lady was very unhappy because her way was blocked going into the restaurant; she became very angry and pushed her way through. She was walking quickly down the aisle when she saw us with all of the beards, long hair and overalls. She was startled and stopped to look for a split second and whirled and left the restaurant immediately. I think she finally realized what the others were looking at. This was way before the hippy/long hair fad had come to our country, and we were an unusual sight for people during that time.

When the reporters came to the school, neither Tobe nor Roy could give them anything to work on from the angle of the frontier existence in the wildwood. They thought that anyone should understand the way a person lived and the things parents, uncles, and cousins talked about, and the things they did. In their innocent way, they had no reason to think that they were different from anybody else.

The hubbub amused them a little. Tobe talked enough to fan their flaming curiosity. Roy said very little, though he was very polite as he smiled his slow smile and listened. It was that refreshing modesty without a single semblance of ego, that warmed those newsmen's hearts. It was to continue to do so until it sold Cut and Shoot to the entire world.

The reporters who met Roy at school followed him, unafraid, into the deep green depths of the limber lost. The newsmen entered another world that they didn't know could co-exist with the streamlined world of the twentieth century. There they met Uncle Roe, and he told them how Cut and Shoot got its name.

"Jeff Mann is a tall skinny fellow, only in his younger days he was a big man. Somebody introduced us the other day, and I said, 'We have known each other a long time.'

"Somebody asked, 'How long have you known each other?' I said, 'Me and Mann gave Cut and Shoot its name.' They all laughed and couldn't figger that out. I said:

"Remember, Mann, when me and George Gandy come along and stopped you and Thomas from that shootin' and all that fightin' and cuttin'?'

"Jeff Mann was in all that fightin'. Three of them Mann's was in it. His daddy was one of 'em . . . the old Man Mann and his brother and his daddy. They were younger men then.

"Mr. Thomas lived over there. Not the Thomas's that live in Cut and Shoot now—that is, Stovall and Collis and them, but another set of Thomas's. They come in here from Georgia, and they had a fall out with the Mann's over a piece of land and they got into a big tush hog fight over it next to Caney Creek. They fell out, and Mann figured he got crooked, and Thomas figured he got crooked. Some of 'em got cut to fussin' over the landline, so they went home and got their guns. They come back 'bout church time and met up close to the church. The church was crossed up with factions, too, and some of the members took sides.

"Me and George Gandy come along there with Crockett Martin, on horse back. So we stopped and said there would be no killin' over no landline in front of no church. And that's how Cut and Shoot got its name. Mr. Alf Morris, a lawyer in Conroe, who tried to settle the landline, said next day it ought to be named Cut and Shoot.

"It all happened over at Caney Creek Bridge, right where Harvey Hazel's daddy lived, and they fell out on the left hand side of the road comin' this way.

"Mr. Morris called it Cut and Shoot. But at first the folks got it mixed up and called it 'Hack and Slash'.

"Everybody purty soon forgot about the row and are good friends today. That's the reason it's so hard to find out how it was named."

Roy on the naming of Cut and Shoot:

I have heard different stories and versions of the same story about how Cut and Shoot got its name. My folks lived here during the naming and remembered it well. There have been several stories about how the community got its name. The first tale makes a good and interesting story.

The state of Texas decided to try and eradicate ticks on livestock. They passed a law in the early 1920s saying that all farm animals had to be dipped. To aid in this massive project, the state built dipping vats all over Texas, including one in the Cut and Shoot area. The livestock were driven into a long fence that cut them off to run through a chute into the dipping vats with water treated with poison to kill ticks. When the livestock went through the chute and jumped into the vat, they went completely under and were soaked with the tick poison. People began to say, "the place where you cut the cows into the fence and run them through the chute." Rather than go through all the explanations, they simply began saying, "Over there at Cut and Shoot."

The dipping project was not successful because it was impossible to dip every tick-carrying animal. Some folks would not comply and others were not able to round up all of their livestock that ran wild through the woods.

Most people agree that this is not [really] what caused the area to be named Cut and Shoot.

Following is part of an article that Robin Montgomery published for the *Conroe Courier* reflecting data from the foremost authority on the naming of the place, Roy's friend and Robin's, Harley Gandy:

> Cut and Shoot, in eastern Montgomery County, is more than just a town of world renown. It is a state of mind reflecting a spirit ready to fight for one's beliefs. Let's explore how the community received its name.
>
> Our story begins in July 1912. One would presume it was hot. The center of the community was a building called a "Community House," a combination church and school. But certain religious denominations were excluded from using the facilities.
>
> Then it happened. July 21, 1912 marked the day that an evangelist of one of the excluded groups scheduled an appearance, bent on conducting a service. Opposing factions emerged and on that July morning, they met, each with weapons concealed within reach. One side was determined to enter the building to have a preaching. The other side was just as determined to prevent said preaching.

As the tension mounted, Jack King, an eight-year-old of one of the families in favor of having the preaching, became frightened. Consequently seeking to "do" something, it is said that he blurted out, "I'm going to cut around the corner and shoot through the bushes."

Fortunately, no cutting and shooting occurred that day. Instead, an uneasy compromise ensued with the visiting evangelist engaging a series of meetings over the next several weeks, but in a shaded spot in the area. His platform was the ground, while the congregation was composed of families seated in their nearby wagons.

Meanwhile, trials were set for the leaders of the respective feuding factions. At one of the gatherings, a witness named Archie Vicks was asked where the confrontation had occurred. Since the place did not have a name, Vick responded that it was "where they had the cutting and shooting scrape." Shortened to "Cut and Shoot", the name stuck.

As reporters converged on Conroe in the aftermath of the Lufkin Golden Gloves tournament, a thousand questions had to be answered. They sought to organize safaris for treks into the Big Thicket. All of them received as much help as the as the startled Conroe folks could give them. To most of them, however, Cut and Shoot was a far-away place spreading over a vast marshy wilderness, inhabited by robust and self-sufficient woodsmen who had risen up during the boom days to become a scourge to the oil field hangers-on who sought to take advantage of them.

One especially inquisitive reporter was George Kellam of the *Fort Worth Star Telegram*. He came to Conroe with a former professional football player, Dewitt Coulter, to serve ostensibly as a photographer, but his real assignment was to act as a bodyguard for Kellam. The pair made their way through the forest to the Harris clearing and was welcomed warmly.

Kellam got his story, and what a story it was. It was voted the best Associated Press Sports Story written in Texas during the year 1950. When he received the award, he was crowned with a coonskin cap, and ever after his colleagues called him, "Cut and Shoot Kellam." He wrote the following story in the Fort Worth *Star-Telegram* under date of February 4. 1950, (reprinted in the Conroe *Courier* February 9, 1950):

> There is really a place called [Cut and Shoot]. There's no post office here, so you won't find it on the map or in any kind of dictionary but the residents of Conroe, ten or twelve miles west, can tell you all about it.
>
> First it is the home of Roy and Tobe Harris, the Harris brothers who won the lightweight and welterweight championships, respectively, in the Lufkin regional Golden Gloves tournament recently. They're going to compete in the State tournament February 15-20 at Fort Worth, Texas.
>
> Secondly, it is one of the few remaining frontier outposts in our highly scientific nation where you still can see with your own eyes the manners and conditions in which our pioneer forefathers lived.

[Cut and Shoot] is about five miles south of highway 105 East from Conroe to Fostoria, 18 miles away. It is located in the southern most fringe of the Sam Houston National Forest, better known in these parts as "The Big Thicket."

[Cut and Shoot] is a community—not a town. However, there is a place in this community, which is considered [Cut and Shoot] proper. It consists of an old abandoned sawmill about 200 yards down a railroad track which intersects the dirt road you travel after turning south off highway 105.

In addition to the abandoned sawmill, there are two log cabins, one of which boasts of two chicken houses, The Tom Outlaws live there.

Just how large a geographical area [Cut and Shoot] community covers no one knows. Some say 30 to 40 square miles.

That's typical of this place. Generalities reign supreme. No one knows exactly how far it is to any place, in or out of the Big Thicket.

According to the Texas Almanac, the Sam Houston Forest is the no. 1 forest in the state of Texas. Though the map shows it runs from a point south of Conroe and Fostoria to a point slightly beyond Huntsville in the north, it actually extends northeast to the Davy Crockett National Forest near Lufkin.

The timber isn't thick along the route but old timers, referring to the Big Thicket, include almost all the country from Conroe to Woodville in the east, north to Lufkin and thence southwest to Huntsville in turn.

The forest is made up of all kinds of trees but pine predominates.

[Cut and Shoot] is located on the northeastern edge of the big Conroe oilfield. There are oil wells and storage tanks within a mile of the Harris log cabin and there is a gas flare in their front yard...

Except for the areas where woodsmen have cleared out trees and built cabins, the undergrowth is so dense it is practically impassable.

There are three creeks, or branches as the woodsmen call them, running through [Cut and Shoot] Community. They are Bear Creek, Panther Creek, and Crystal Creek. The Harris's live near Crystal Creek. It runs three quarters of a mile from their house and is liberally dotted with quicksand.

There are two stories about how [Cut and Shoot] got its name. Both agree that it is derived from methods of arguing peculiar to this community, but one says it resulted from a dispute between two factions over a church problem and the other insists it came from extra-curricular activities which accompanied political rallies in the early 1900s.

[Cut and Shoot] is in Montgomery County and one of our guides, J. T. Montgomery, principal of Wm. B. Travis Junior High School in Conroe, is a direct descendant of the family after which the county is named.

All of the woodsmen here wear coonskin caps—made from the real McCoy. [A close friend that they call "Armadillo"] makes the caps.

The residents of [Cut and Shoot] aren't worried about income taxes, strikes, H-bombs, or communism. The

Harris's, for example, live in a two acre clearing. About one-third of it is in cultivation. There they raise what vegetables they need. They have "a herd of hogs," several head of cattle and chickens.

If more meat is desired, the forest abounds in game such as deer, coon, fish, and rabbit. These people recognize no hunting season but they kill only when they need food—not for sport.

The Harris's own "bout 29" hound dogs. Only ten of them were around the house. "Rest of 'em are out on a coon hunt I reckon," Henry explained.

Morally, these people are sincere, honest, and simple in their ways and full of a backwoods-type humor that would be the envy of an ulcer-haunted businessman.

They leave the Thicket, "bout once or twice a year" for flour, salt, and the like, but otherwise the forest is their grocery store.

"Back in the old days, 10 or 15 years ago, all the men folks used to go off back into the Thicket, find a small clearing and stage fights to determine the bare knuckle champion of the Big Thicket," Montgomery said.

"Henry," Montgomery added, "was defending champion of the Big Thicket for many years and it's this knowledge and background of fighting he uses to teach Tobe and Roy how to fight."

[Henry] Harris, who is a very intelligent man though not too well educated, emphasizes that his people don't go 'round lookin' for trouble, but when trouble comes it gets a warm reception in [Cut and Shoot].

The boys are very intelligent and attend Conroe Senior High School occasionally—once or twice a week, that is. Their teachers say the boys always show up when it's time for a test and make from 85 to 95 on it. Tobe will graduate this June and Henry hopes his boxing will enable him to get a college scholarship somewhere.

Uncle Bob and . . .Armadillo are the most interesting of the family.

As we approached the Harris cabin (had to walk the last mile—no road) Uncle Bob was in a supine position on the front porch clad in new blue overalls he wore to the Lufkin tournament, but devoid of footwear.

The children were playing in the yard barefooted and bareheaded. They disappeared into the house as we approached. Henry stepped out of the house wearing his coonskin cap and, along with Uncle Bob, gave us a warm greeting. . .

We moved toward the ring made of four pine sapling posts and three strands of rope, which at one time had been wrapped in burlap sacks, accompanied by Uncle Bob, Tobe and Roy.

Minutes later up rode . . .Armadillo clad in cowboy boots, blue jeans, homemade buckskin jacket, coonskin cap, and resting a worn 22 caliber pump action rifle across his knee. He approached warily.

"Git down off that hoss, put away the gun and come ovah heah and meet these people," shouted Henry.

Armadillo reacted with the respect and quickness of movement expected by a former bareknuckle champion of the Big Thicket.

"Armadillo", explained Uncle Bob, "ain't got no teeth. He got 'em knocked out fightin' Tobe and Roy."

Uncle Bob said he lived "12, 13, maybe fo'teen miles ovah theah," waving his arm in the northerly direction. He had a string of camps that run approximately 40 miles toward Lufkin. He moves from one to the other, hunting, fishing, keeping track of hogs while they feed.

There is one other Harris brother. He's Uncle Jack. Uncle Jack hasn't cut his hair in years. They say it hangs down below his shoulders and he sports a long curly handlebar type mustache, all in white. Uncle Jack wasn't around at the time however.

Henry pointed out the torn down auto engine which Tobe and Roy used for weight lifting. The boys picked up the cylinder heads, weight about 55 to 60 pounds each, hoisted them above their heads and held them there several minutes while posing for a picture. They didn't strain a muscle either.

There are two stories regarding their physical hardiness that make you wonder how far they might go in the state tournament.

Their dad had an attack of appendicitis several years ago," Montgomery says, "The appendix burst but Henry still refused to be 'cut-in'. He 'turned black as pitch tar' but his excellent physical condition pulled him through."

A lot of things in Texas are amazing, the most amazing of which are Texans when they become amazed at themselves. Surely they must revel in being amazingly different. That was one reason the Cut and Shoot clan suddenly found itself deep in the heart of every Texan; another reason was the luster that shone from the personalities of Tobe and Roy.

From El Paso to Texarkana, Cut and Shoot climbed onto the headlines. Coon commanded bigger captions than did the Kremlin's boycott of the United Nations. Besides that, his picture, along with an array of his fellow Cut and Shooters, hogged the newspaper space and caused dainty little coming-out debutantes to wad up the papers and fling them on the floor in a much harder way than Roy could have ever floored an opponent. The amazed editor of the Conroe *Courier* wrote that the Cut and Shoot brothers were getting more publicity than the atom bomb.

Kellam's newspaper, the Fort Worth *Star-Telegram* represented the National Golden Glove organization in Texas. Therefore, all regional champions from over the state came to Fort Worth each February to slug it out with an amateur eagerness in the massive Will Rogers Memorial Coliseum. The laboratory tests made in that roped–in crucible were never lacking for simon-pure guinea pigs who were ready and willing to give their all for the science of boxing, provided of course, a championship crown dangled for the winner at the end of the experiments.

Flem Hall, sports editor of the *Star-Telegram* and kingpin of all that appertained to the Golden Gloves in Texas, ordered a command performance at the state tournament of as many of the Cut and Shoot clansmen as could be rounded up. His underlings heated up the telephone wires to Conroe, exhorting the school officials to help them carry out the assignment.

"We are prepared to 'foot the bill' for a week in Fort Worth," they said,' for as many of the Harris clan as you folks down there can bring up here."

Fort Worth, most times called "Cow Town," prides itself on being the city "Where the West Begins", and most of its citizens have a picturesqueness of speech that compares rather unfavorably with the grammatical niceties of the scions at Oxford.

"We would be pleased," they said, "if you folks would hunt them up and do your best to get them up here."

Receiving the call was Dr. Hulon N. Anderson, the legendary Superintendent of the Conroe Independent School System. Dr. Anderson had seen much in his storied career and had been very supportive of the Conroe boxing program and its colorful atmosphere. Hence, on hanging up the phone, he could not help giving forth a little chuckle as he muttered, "Poor reporters, gracious to the extreme though they be, they do not realize the magnitude of the excitement they are inviting to their city. "

They certainly didn't, but a few days later they were to find out.

Chapter X

WOODSMEN IN COW-TOWN

According to the seed almanac, the sun rose on Tuesday morning, February 14, 1950 at exactly a quarter until seven.

"There she come an' we be hard nigh on a million miles from home roost." That was Armadillo's greeting to a gradual sunrise approximately thirty miles north of Conroe.

"I guess Little Henry is milking the cows about now", said Henry thinking of his family, "and Gladys and the girls are fixing breakfast."

Armadillo now had the sunny side of the front seat of the northbound mechanism that once was an automobile, and he was busily adjusting his coonskin cap to shut out the rising sunrays.

Twenty miles farther up the highway, Uncle Bob became homesick. His long bewhiskered face was sad. "Henry, I be determined to go back home now," he said.

No one in the car was surprised that he said it. They kept quiet. The only thing audible was the clatter of tappet in the well-worn motor and a cutout roar from the sagging muffler of the ancient vehicle driven by J. T. Montgomery, the school principal.

"Is this Fort Worth?" Bob pleaded, pointing up ahead to a hamlet two hundred miles south of their destination.

"No doubt, it are it," surmised Cousin Coon in as hopeful a way as he could muster.

They approached the town and drove through it. After a roar and a backfire north of town, Uncle Bob moaned, "Henry, I'm ready to go back home . . .right now!"

Coon reminded him of the free demijohns sealed over with government labels waiting for them in Fort Worth.

Uncle Bob unconsciously licked his lips and murmured weakly, "Spect I'm gonna be a mite homesick soon, if Coon hasn't figgered right. I'd still rather go home though."

He slipped a bottle from his hip pocket and unscrewed the lid. Henry's face took on a tolerant expression. Then he looked away.

Far up the road they stopped to stretch. Truck drivers slowed down to look at the transposed frontiersmen while more anemic motorists fearfully stamped their gas pedals to the floorboard.

"There's no hog tracks in the gulley," spoke Coon as he examined the rim of the road ditch.

"Reckon as how folks up this way make a poor kind of livin'," replied Bob.

Coon scratched his head. He looked at the great vans speeding down the highway with pretty printing on their sides.

"Those things sure could haul some amount o' hogs," he reasoned. "Roy, what does the writin' say?"

"That one says 'potato chips,'" explained Roy.

"Sure would take a heap o' grubbin' to fill her up," Coon said. "Poor ol' fingernails would get downright sassy next to the quick 'a fore you took that many 'taters out of the ground."

A sleek automobile containing a man, his wife and two Wald-eyed children slowed to a stop on the opposite highway shoulder from the parked jalopy. All four, as Coon remarked later, "looked long in the face like a horse."

Armadillo strode slowly across the concrete highway toward them. Drivers of cars and trucks disregarded the centerline as they sat down on their horns and brakes. A late model convertible settled in the road ditch that Coon was examining. He ran through the water to help the occupants.

"Hey there Mister, your ol' hoss kinda shied, didn't he?" shouted Coon. "Light down and come up on the bank. Where you be from? I am up here from Cut and Shoot. Name's Coon."

The man helped his girlfriend from the convertible. He was mad, as he was wet. Rudely, he refused any assistance from the gallant Coon.

"Get out of my way," he stormed. "I'll sue you . . .In fact I think I'll . . ." He shut up when he saw the bulk of Henry and Bob and got a better look at Coon.

"Have some dog," Coon offered as he extended a pig liver sandwich to the crest-fallen owner of the convertible.

Armadillo had reached the other side of the highway leaving its lanes open now for straightaway traffic. The friendly lad tipped his coonskin cap to the lady and offered the man "a chaw of tobacco." He bent down and grinned a wide nicotine grin at the two children cowering on the opposite side of the back seat.

"How far be it twist here and up to Fort Worth?" He asked.

The man didn't answer but sat there in dumb astonishment at the size of the pig sticker Armadillo was using to carve off a corner of his tobacco plug.

"Don't guess you must a'heared me, suh," the backwoods boy said softly. Then, not thinking about the knife he now had firmly gripped by its handle, he raised his voice to a demanding pitch. "How far in tarnation be it to Fort Worth?"

That was the picture the highway patrolmen saw when they eased to a stop. An officer promptly disarmed Armadillo.

"What is your name, son?" he asked.

"Armadillo," was the brief reply.

"You look more like a coon with that thing you have on your head," said the officer.

"That's him over yonder," volunteered Armadillo, pointing across the highway to Coon.

The man who had swerved his convertible into the road-ditch to miss the jaywalking Armadillo, came over to complain to the officer. He gestured to his woebegone automobile, then to the, so he thought, hideous Armadillo. He raged and demanded that the officer arrest the irresponsible hillbilly for that brash boy's own good, and for the good of society as a whole. Too, his own hurt feelings needed soothing, and there was the matter of monetary retribution for damages done to his car.

"How for a piece be it up to Fort Worth?" interrupted Armadillo. "Uncle Bob gotta have some labeled whiskey. All he got now is some in a bottle in his hind pocket.

The officer smiled and walked over to Coon, thinking he was Bob. "Give me the bottle in your pocket," he demanded, still smiling.

The quick-witted Coon immediately sized up the ticklish situation. He knew he had to stall for time and at the same time let Bob know to dispose of the bottle.

"Where you folks get your 'taters 'round here?" He was talking loud enough for everybody to hear him. "Truck come 'long here while ago with 'nough 'taters to make a creek full of 'tater beer. Guess ya'll don't make your taters up in beer though 'cause it's not legal up here, and you'd land down to the county jail, and you never would hear a sloppin' pig grunt again. Know if you had any of the stuff you'd chunk her in the hind seat of somebody else's car before you got real, sure nuff, put in jail."

That's exactly what Bob did and the evidence soon rode off with a stranger.

On the evening side of that afternoon, the backwoodsmen puttered up to the front of Westbrook Hotel in downtown Fort Worth. There, television, radio, and newspaper representatives pounced upon them. A crowd gathered on the sidewalk to see the celebrities from Coon Country about whom they had read and heard so much during the previous fortnight.

Through the narrow rift in that thronging mass of curious humans in front of the hotel shivered a yellow, shaggy dog that made his limber-legged way to Roy.

The serious minded youth paid no attention to the broadside of questions propounded in his direction by the eager newsmen. His attention was focused on the puppy. He had lifted it into his arms and snuggled it to his bosom.

"This dog is lost like me," he said to Montgomery. "He is far from home where folks soon's kick him as me if he don't please them. Once I read 'bout Abe Lincoln when he was a far piece from home and was lonesome like me and this little dog. Mr. Lincoln said:

> "I find myself far from home and surrounded by thousand. I now see before me those who are strangers to me . . . still we are bound together in Christianity, civilization . . .

Roy stopped there. He wondered if the people there thought he was civilized. The puppy reared up and clawed at Roy's coonskin cap. Roy was well pleased.

"Henry," he said. "This puppy's gotta be mine. Is it all right with you?"

Henry scratched his beard, wondering about the boy and his dog in a hotel in a strange city when boxing, and boxing alone, should be the only order of business and pleasure.

Finally, Henry responded, "We have enough dogs, but I guess if no one claims him you can take him in."

"Aren't there be plenty of dogs in Cut and Shoot?" Henry asked.

Henry was wise enough to fall back on another Abraham Lincoln quote when he gave Roy permission to keep the puppy: "I'll put my faith in Providence, and let my whiskers grow. " he said, while the television cameras ground out the record.

The surge of people on the sidewalk pushed the country bred travelers into the hotel lobby.

Montgomery tried to register the band of frontiersmen at the hotel desk.

"All of the rooms are occupied," said the bright-eyed girl at the registration desk.

"We are up from Cut and Shoot and need a place to stretch out," declared Uncle Bob. He looked around the lobby for evidence of bonded alcohol when he said it.

They finally persuaded the girl to telephone the sports desk of the Fort Worth *Star Telegram* to verify their reservations. Receiving confirmation, she told the shaken bellhop, "Take them to the sixth floor."

When they had been shown to their rooms, the bellhop politely asked, after he had filled a wooden bucket with ice cubes, if there were anything else they needed.

Bob asked for some bonded Bourbon. He didn't know what Bourbon was but he wanted some after the bellhop told him it came in bottles and was good for what he wanted it for.

Armadillo was afraid because he knew, from experience, exactly what was going to happen to Bob when that merry man got hold of a corn liquor bottle. He was further afraid because he had drawn Bob as his roommate.

Later they went to the elaborate hotel grill for their evening meal. Bob ordered a steak "that long," and he measured the width of the table with his hands.

Distinguished diners at the other tables had multiple expressions on their faces. Bob's coonskin cap covered half his face.

"I see you eat crawfish tails, too," said Armadillo to a society matron at the next table who had an order of shrimp before her. She disdained to even look up.

"A wondrous lot of folks slop in this eatin' house and don't slurp up all their grub," surmised Coon as he got up and walked to the third or fourth table to his left. The foursome who had been eating there had just left, so Coon gathered up the steak bones and flung them on the floor for Roy's newly found puppy. The management swallowed hard. Their uncouth guest might be the talk of "Cow Town," but being host to them in the hotel was pushing their tolerance to the breaking point.

Bob opened his pocketknife, sharpened it on his brogan sole, and went to work on his steak before the waiter who was serving it could remove his hand from the platter. He sliced long strips the entire length of the sirloin and forked them, in dangling ribbons, into his ceiling turned mouth. He wadded up the napkin in his whiskers and dragged his forearm from elbow to finger knuckles across his face, much like a bull-fiddler draws his bow across the strings.

Roy sat in rigid silence. He wasn't the least bit embarrassed, but neither was he completely at ease. Before he ate, however, he adopted a policy of watchful waiting. The studious boy didn't cast side long glances at the dining strangers to sneak previews of the proper table etiquette he wished to employ in tussling with his own meal. He boldly leveled his eyes at them in an earnest contrite way, that caused the people he observed to smile back warmly at him.

Roy's mom taught and expected good table manners from all her children. This prompted Roy to think, "These people don't eat any different from Gladys. They are just plain, polite, good folks eating their groceries real nice like. Bet they'd eat like Bob if they spent a week with him in the woods on a hog hunt. Some of them might even eat like Bob on a Sunday picnic, if they were real hungry."

Roy was losing his thicket vocabulary, even in his thinking. After all, he was a high school junior and making excellent grades in his English classes. He turned to his supper with no misgivings. His feeding kinsmen were no different to him from the well-mannered city people. All he wanted to do was to learn the rules that governed the world outside of Cut and Shoot. Not that the homespun way was to be replaced by primness and pseudosophistication, but his father had told him to be like John Wesley, that is, "mix a little learning with plain horse sense."

That night the country gentry from the rain forest were escorted to the coliseum to watch Goose Tatum and the Harlem Globe Trotters. After the game, they returned to the hotel to rest for the boxing bouts that were to begin the next night. Bob and Armadillo returned with them, but they didn't rest.

All that night they wandered through the city streets, and wherever they wandered, a crowd of curious followed. A group of muggers tried to rob them, but changed their mind when Armadillo flashed his pig sticker.

The next day Bob wouldn't let Armadillo sleep. At the fights that night when Tobe and Roy were swinging away with the crowd's thunderous approval,

Bob spent his time keeping his boon companion from snoring.

"Why'd you come here this far anyhow if you're gonna sleep like ol' sow bedded up 'neath a clay root? Tobe don' lost his fight and Roy's havin' a disturbin' fracas up there now with that wildcat he's done tied on to."

Bob tried to preach those words into Armadillo's nodding head, while tossing it like a lion flaring his mane, and gave forth a blood curdling yell that pierced its way above ten thousand cheers welling up in the arena.

When the referee raised Roy's hand in victory, Bob slapped Armadillo so hard between the shoulder blades that he later had to carry the limp form of the young forester over his shoulder through the milling thousands to the antique car on the parking lot.

Back at the hotel, Bob permitted Coon to carry Armadillo through the dignified lobby to the elevator. Bob chose to linger outside with his hundreds of city friends. If Walt Whitman had of been there when Bob stepped jovially from the car, he no doubt would have said:

> "A tall figure stepped out, paused leisurely on the sidewalk, look'd up at the granite walls and looming architecture of the grand old hotel . . . then, after a relieving stretch of arms and legs, turn'd 'round for

over a minute to slowly and good-humoredly scan the vast and silent crowds . . .He look'd with curiosity upon the immense sea of faces, and the sea of faces return'd the look with similar curiosity. In both, there was a dash of comedy, almost farce . . . ."

On the sixth floor of the Westbrook in rooms allocated to the Cut and Shooters, whose kinsmen had joined them from Oklahoma and Arkansas, a victory celebration for the fortunate Roy was in full swing. Roy and Wildman were asleep in a room down the hall. Armadillo was further down the hall with his door thumb-bolted from the inside. He was utterly exhausted and didn't want Uncle Bob to disturb him when that fun loving rascal came barreling off the streets in the early morning hours.

If there were any roosters in Fort Worth, they were crowing when the party ended. The elevator operators gradually ceased their up and down bobbing. Room service sighed in relief. House detectives went off the alert. The tired hotel was at rest at last, enthralled in its memories of other days when whooping cowboys rode into town to revel up and down her corridor.

Then suddenly, pandemonium jarred a hundred people out of dreamland. The sixth floor of the Westbrook took on a semblance of a high suite in the shaking walls of Jericho when the Israelites surrounded and conquered that Biblical town. A blistering barrage of neo-American language welled and surged and spiced the shaking.

Uncle Bob had returned, dog-tired from his prowling, only to find the door to his room bolted shut.

Henry, in his long-handles, looked sixty yards down the hallway to where his boisterous brother stood with his head bowed in dejection. Every door between the brothers was open. From each door protruded, like a turtle's head from its shell, a startled faced, drawn-eyed occupant. Bob was furious.

"Stick in your heads or come out of your holes an' look at me like a man before fore I bust your heads like a long row o' watermelons," yelled the raging Bob.

Doors on both sides of the hallway slammed like dominoes falling when they are lined up close together in a horizontal position. Bob swung up and kicked out the transom. In a splintering of glass, he landed on his back in the room. He rolled and roared.

Henry and Coon and the clan and their kinfolks dashed to Armadillo's rescue in their underwear. They knocked the door down and found Bob holding Armadillo by his ankles from the window. The lad said later that he "waked up an' the world done turned wrong-side-up in Fort Worth."

Roy lost a close decision to Billy Burkhead the next night, but before that happened Montgomery and Henry had to travel five hundred miles, in the pokey car, from Fort Worth to Cut and Shoot and back, to carry Bob home.

The *Star-Telegram* bigwigs had insisted that Bob be banished back to the underbrush before he inadvertently involved them in a lawsuit. They had read of other days when two Indian chiefs, Quanah Parker and Yellow Bear, arrived in Fort Worth and registered at the Pickwick Hotel. That night, Yellow Bear died because Parker had prowled until midnight then blew out the gas light when he went to bed, instead of turning it off.

It was raining in the rain forest when the old car reached Bob's home. He hadn't said a word during the five-hour trip from Fort Worth. He didn't say a word when he kicked open the car door, but went directly to his cow horn hanging by the water shelf. After standing straight and raising his arms to greet the forest, he put his lips to the horn to send musical peals ringing through the thicket. The music hitting home in their canine hearts, his score of dogs came whining and whimpering to sit on their haunches in a circle around their master.

At last Bob took the horn from his lips. A tear or two mingled on his cheeks with the raindrops when he extended his hand to the uplifted forepaws of the only true friends he knew.

"Hope Roy wins tonight," he said.

He blew another blast on the hunting horn and the dogs followed him into the forest. He hadn't slept in fifty hours. It might be fifty more before he curled up in a hollow log to hibernate.

Fortunately the sports world is more tolerant for the loser than are the critics in most any other field of human endeavor. No doubt they are that way because they see a loser every time they see a winner. Naturally they love a winner who claims the victory through honest effort according to the rules. That kind of winner is also applauded in all of the other subdivisions of our complicated social structure, but only the sports world has mercy on those who strive and fail. Certainly they don't cater to the theory of the devil take the hindmost.

Tobe and Roy were spared the sting of humiliation because sports lovers were their critics. Had this not been their lot they could have read headlines like "The Cut and Shoot Bubble has burst" or "How Sloppy Can a Hog Boy Be?" To the everlasting credit of the sports fraternity, nothing like that appeared in any Texas newspaper. Just the results received publication.

Cut and Shoot swallowed up the colorful clansmen. They hadn't wanted to leave the leafy forest in the first place. Since they had been persuaded to go against their better judgment and join the city fighters, however, they resolved to thrive for a year on the experience they took home with them.

A few weeks later the boys blasted their way through the Conroe tournament. That summer Roy won the Junior Olympic middleweight championship in Houston. He and Tobe farmed the land and trained.

The next February they elected to go to Bryan to the Regional Tournament of Golden Gloves. The Chamber of Commerce of that city gave a downtown parade in honor of Cut and Shoot. A coon was tied to a leash. Following the coon were a dozen dogs, also on leashes. Other rustic motifs swelled the festivities to prove the welcome of the heralded Harris's. The culminating climax came when the Sheriff presented Armadillo with the key to the County Jail.

Tobe, Roy and Wildman easily won their way back to the State Tournament. In Fort Worth, Roy lost to Eugene Cooper. The second trip however, was not quite as disastrous as had been the first one.

The next year, 1952, Roy won the state middleweight championship and in winning it, he had the satisfaction of earning a technical knockout victory, in the semi-finals, over the same Eugene Cooper who had stopped him the year before.

A new day had dawned in the wide, wide world that Roy Harris had recently discovered. With character and determination and a wicked left hook, he ventured forth to conquer it.

Chapter XI

FULFILLMENT

Roy sat on his porch steps in the darkening evening. His wife, who had been his childhood sweetheart, graced a lounging chair on the porch. She was talking softly to his Grandmother Murray.

"Roy has been training so hard for the fight with Willie Pastrano," she sighed with mingled anxiety and relief. "It's a shame his eye was cut this afternoon and the fight was called off."

Mrs. Murray thought awhile. Her heart of hearts contained an unbounded love for this grandson who looked and conducted himself so much like her deceased husband's people.

"God's will be done," she replied. "I never wanted Roy to fight in the first place, but Saint John wrote in the New Testament: 'The Son can do nothing of himself, but what he seeth the Father do; for what things so ever he doeth, these also doeth the Son likewise.'

"Those words," she explained, "were meant for God the Father and His Son, but they can also apply to Henry and Roy."

Roy said nothing, as usual. He sat on the steps and basked in the warm love of his wife and grandmother. Across the alligator pond, close by, was the home of his nativity. A porch full of clansmen, as usual, were sprawled there listening to his father expound on a hundred different subjects. Roy saw his loving mother strolling down the trail. It made him happy as she walked up the steps ruffled his hair in a very tender way, then sat down by her mother, Mrs. Murray.

Gladys was a typical mother for her day. She managed her home and children while her husband worked to make the living. She was the disciplinarian of the family. What she said was the law. If one of us children needed a spanking, she took care of that problem as soon as possible and never waited for Henry. We did as she encouraged, as we knew our rear ends would be blistered if we did not. She was firm and fair with her discipline. She was good hearted and kind and would give her life to protect her children. She was slow to anger, but when she got mad, she was really mad.

We had oatmeal every morning as that is what Gladys thought we should have to start the day. She was into healthy eating and healthy foods, before eating healthy was even popular. Some of her specialties were chicken and dumplings, chicken fried steak and chicken fried chicken. She would also fix something called "Mulligan stew". It had beef and veggies cooked together in a broth served with cornbread, and we always looked forward to her serving it. She cooked and prepared what we grew and raised. Food was always plentiful for us. We had vegetables of all kinds, chickens and eggs, milk, buttermilk, butter, beef and pork. My sisters learned to cook at an early age from my mother who was an excellent cook.

In the spring and early summer, she spent a lot of her time putting up produce that we grew in the garden and field. Since we had no electricity, we had no freezer. She put the food up in jars. The vegetables she canned were mostly peas, beans, corn, tomatoes and okra. She made pickles out of cucumbers as well as a lot of chow-chow. She used a pressure cooker to cook the food over a natural gas stove. The whole family helped when Gladys said it was time to can the vegetables. It was hard work for us all.

As Gladys joined Mrs. Murray and Jean that cool afternoon, they talked of many things that women usually discuss. Since mothers and wives and grandmothers usually have a lot in common, they centered their low-toned conversation on the thinker on the doorstep.

Roy summarizes the story of his life with Jean:

Jean and I met while we were in Travis Junior High School waiting for the school bus to take us home after school. This was in 1947, and I was fifteen years of age and in the 9th grade, and she was in the 7th grade. We did not ride the same bus, but we all waited in the same bus line to catch the different busses. Both of us lived in the Cut and Shoot area. We were not particularly good friends at this time, but we were acquaintances. I was busy with going to school and boxing, and Jean kept busy helping her dad in his nursery business. I remember that I must have liked her even then, as I picked on her and even flirted a little. I wanted her to like me.

I went on to Conroe High School. Jean finished Travis Junior High in Conroe and went to Conroe High School for her 9th and 10th grades. During her 10th year and my senior year, we had a class together. It was a cooking class taught by Mrs. Georgia Watson. I remember that we had to eat everything we cooked, and I quickly found out that I was not born to be a cook. I also found out that I really liked Jean. Since I had neither transportation nor money, dating was out of the question. So we remained friends in class only.

Jean transferred to a church school in Owossa, Michigan for part of her high school years. We had no contact with each other while she was away. She graduated from Conroe High School in 1952.

Fate finally came to my aid. In October of 1954, my sister, Helen, wanted to go to Francis Miller's 16th birthday party, and I was the brother who reluctantly provided the transportation to take his sister. I had intended to drop her off and come back and pick her up later to take her home but my plans changed.

As soon as I got her there, I saw Jean. She was in the car with one of her friends, Lavonne Miller. I kicked my professional flirting operation into full gear as soon as I saw Jean. I began to try to get a date with her. Everything I could think of, she vetoed as she was not available or did not have time for me. Finally, I asked her if she went to church, as going to church was one of her excuses not to go with me. I was told that she did go every Saturday at a certain time. I finally got her to agree to allow me to attend church with her. The rest is history, as the old saying goes. We married on September 24, 1955. I had found my soul mate and did not want to lose her.

We had a small wedding in her yard at her home. She wore a long white dress, and I wore my only suit. Her sister, Lela, was her maid of honor and Johnny Hopkins was my best man. Barbara Jones sang at our wedding. She later worked in Hollywood. Her circle of friends included Lorne Green, Clint Eastwood, Don Knots and other famous movie stars. After the wedding, we drove in our tin can/old shoe decorated car to Cleveland where we spent our one night honeymoon! I had a fight coming up three days later, so we could not go far.

As Jean, Gladys and Mrs. Murray visited, Roy stroked the adhesive tape that bound his injured eye. It wasn't sore yet because it hadn't had time to get that way. A whippoorwill made the night sweeter with his sudden greeting from the far side of the alligator pond as a flicker of celestial light above the pine trees to the east betrayed the nightly thunderheads slipping, specter like, up the far away Trinity River.

"It's raining over there on the river," Grandmother Murray observed. "Does it nearly every night." She had a far-away look in her eyes.

"Me and your pa," she intended for Gladys to hear her, "used to sit, when we were the age of Jean and Roy, just like we're sitting now, and watch the lightening in the summer clouds and listen to the whippoorwills. He was the exact image of the lad.

He was quiet too—just like Roy is, thought a lot and encouraged my input when he had a big decision to make. He was a wonderful husband."

Roy eased himself from where he sat and walked with measured steps behind the home place to the trail that led to one of his favorite spots, a little pine grove. He thought he walked alone, but his wife walked in the shadows behind him.

He sat down near the place he had stood eight years before after his fight in Conroe and listened to the string band play "Wildwood Flower." Those intervening years flooded before his eyes.

Seventy nine amateur battles, four times Golden Gloves champion of Texas: middleweight in 1952, light heavyweight in 1953, and heavyweight in 1954 and 1955; Championship after championship in Amateur Athletic Union, A.A.U. eliminations until finally he had won the A.A.U. heavyweight championship of the South. Before that, he had won one welterweight and two middleweight Junior Olympic crowns and six regional Golden Gloves championships.

In Chicago, sickness had plagued him. Each of the four times he lifted himself to the threshold of national honors, influenza gripped him. No one ever knew it, but it was a difficult thing for a boy, running through the steaming southern swamps, to fight his way through regional and state tournaments and end up in the frigid north in the dead of winter, without being floored by a cold germ along the way.

He had fought in the windy city in suffering silence. In 1952, he lost his first fight. The next year he advanced to the quarterfinals.

In 1954, he tried harder to prepare himself for the inevitable showdown with the flu than he did for his gloved opponents. Each morning and evening he took an ice water bath in the open air. It worked. He felt good in Chicago and battled his way to the semi-finals. The cold changes in the climatic conditions had been licked. He came home to prepare for the finals that were to be held a few weeks later. The abrupt changes floored him, however, and he was unable to return to Chicago.

In 1955, he was sick before he left Fort Worth but went on to Chicago anyway, to yet another major milestone in his career.

Roy lay on the pine straw beneath the sighing pine trees thinking of that milestone. Jean had joined him. She knew her handsome husband was alone in his thoughts. She sat close to where he lay and eased her back against the smooth bark of a yellow pine tree. She didn't want to say anything to break the spell. She only chose to slip her right hand into that terrible left fist that had put pugilist from coast to coast into sudden sleep.

The tingling tenderness of Jean's touch had caused him to close his eyes. Instead of interrupting his reverie, he found it blissfully intensified, and the many nice things that had happened to him surged in his brain from out of the past. His warm friend, Bill Van Fleet of the *Star-Telegram* staff who was perennial chaperon of the Texas Golden Gloves teams to Chicago, had written a nice article about him after the 1955 national tournament.

As he lay with his eyes closed and with the moonbeams playing about his face, he thought about that fast loyal friend and of the article he had written. He had read it so many times because it personified his innermost feelings. He almost had it memorized.

Van Fleet wrote in the Fort Worth *Star-Telegram*, March 5, 1955:

> Roy Harris won the Joe Louis sportsmanship award at the Chicago Goldens by maintaining calm under what he later confessed was hotly vexing disappointment.
>
> The people who make the award undoubtedly picked the [Cut and Shoot] heavyweight at the instant his quarterfinals bout was stopped and a technical knockout awarded to Dale Volberg of Sioux City, Iowa.
>
> Roy was six-lengths or so in front when he was floored by a long punch to the ear. When he arose, the referee looked into his eyes, decided he was addled, and stopped the bout. There were but 15 seconds left in the third and last round.

"I wasn't hurt. I've been hit lots harder than that. Billy Burton hurt me a lot more last fall in an intercity bout. And that fellow (Volberg) never would have hit me again," Roy said Friday when he came through Fort Worth on his way to Sam Houston State College where he is a junior agricultural student.

" People tell me I always look wild-eyed in the ring. I guess I do but I wasn't hurt," he continued. "But it was my fault for getting hit in the first place. I thought Volberg was too slow to hit me."

At any rate, Harris made no commotion, accepted the referee's decision and walked smilingly from the ring. The award people had their man.

Roy thought of his college days. He had finished Conroe High School in 1951 and enrolled at Tarleton State College because Tobe had gone there the year before. After one semester he transferred to Texas A&M. That school, like Tarleton State, was too expensive for a boy with only a few dollars in his pocket—dollars earned the hard way in the cornfields and rough necking in the oil field. He transferred to a college closer to home.

The years at Sam Houston State College in Huntsville were filled with monotonous travel. Each morning, after doing the many chores, he ran for an hour through the wilderness. Then, still before daylight, after a slow deliberate breakfast and a last minute review of his lessons, he would crank his antique jalopy and drive forty miles, many times through the rain, to his classes.

There were cows to be milked in the evenings. Many times his father had hogs and cattle in the pens that needed his attention. Countless other odd jobs occupied his limited spare time: stove wood splitting, fence mending, clearing out underbrush, fighting wood fires, doctoring animals for screwworms, and on and on, almost into infinity. Still he found time to study his textbooks and to perfect himself in the skills of his chosen profession.

He smiled there in the moonlight when he thought of the B average he had maintained throughout those trying, yet happy years. Another sweeter thought possessed him causing him to open his eyes and squeeze his wife's hand. The thoughts that consumed him at that moment were the most wonderful in his life.

It was immediately after he had enrolled for his senior year at Sam Houston, that he had married the girl who now sat serenely by his side.

Gloria Jean Groce, a native of Cut and Shoot, was from a pioneer Texas family. One of her ancestral uncles had contributed his part in an immeasurable way, to the success of Sam Houston's Army in its preparation for the Battle of San Jacinto.

Roy grasped her hand a little tighter and turned his eyes toward her. He focused his gaze to the left of the pine grove to where a massive rustic training camp loomed in the dim outline against the darkened forest. It hadn't been there during his glorious amateur years.

All of his training had been done in those days in Henry's front yard with Tobe. The training camp by the pine grove was a symbol of his later advancement in the professional boxing world.

Roy comments on his pre-professional days:

While I was in high school I began boxing for Sam Houston State Teachers College. My old junior high coach, Glen Buffaloe, was now boxing coach there and allowed me to fight against college boxers. This let me get more experience by fighting different fighters from different places. I began to learn more about the other college boys and how they were able to go to school. I learned that most of the other boys were as financially poor as I was and had to work and pay their own way, but they managed. I decided then that if they could do it, I could and began to think seriously about it. During summers in high school I went to work for different oil companies to earn money to save for tuition, books and transportation to college.

After graduation from high school, I started college at a branch of Texas A&M, John Tarleton at Stephenville, where I was in the ROTC (Reserve Officer Training Corps). I went one semester and transferred to A&M. I was boxing at the time and had won the

Regional Golden Gloves at Brownwood and the State Golden Gloves tournament in Ft. Worth and on to the National Golden Gloves in Chicago. I was gone from school about a month. The officials at A&M decided that I could not continue to attend Texas A&M because I had missed too many days of school for boxing. They told me that I had to choose between boxing and going to college and could not do both there. They would not consider any possibility of my continuing that semester at A&M. So, I moved back home and went to work; I worked six months in the oil field and attempted college again, this time at Sam Houston.

I approached Sam Houston State Teachers College about going to school there. Dr. Harmon Lowman, the President of Sam Houston, welcomed me there and told me that he was glad I was doing so well in boxing. I enrolled again in ROTC, which had just started at Sam Houston. Dr. Lowman continued supporting my going to school as well as my boxing. I changed my major from Engineering to Vocational Agriculture when I entered Sam.

I lost my first fight in the nationals in the National Golden Gloves Tournament in Chicago in 1952, although I thought that I had whipped the boy who won. This was in the middleweight division. The next year I advanced to the quarterfinals, still in middleweight. In 1954, I advanced to the semifinals. The finals were a few weeks later, but I was unable to return for the finals as I had a bad cold and lost by default.

In 1955 we returned to Chicago once again. The fighter who was to represent Texas in the heavyweight division did not want to go to Chicago. The boxing officials of Texas asked me to go as a heavyweight and let another light heavyweight fight in the Texas light heavyweight division. I was a light heavyweight fighter, fighting heavyweight in Chicago. In fact, I had to weigh in there with my clothes on to qualify as heavyweight. I advanced to the semi-finals. I was clearly winning the fight until the last few seconds of the last round when my opponent hit me with a right hand and knocked me down. When I got up, in less than four seconds, the referee stopped the fight and awarded it to the other fighter. I was not hurt, and the referee made a bad mistake by stopping the fight. One of the judges criticized him for stopping the fight just seconds before the end, and he thought it was plain to see that I was up and ready to fight with only a few seconds left.

I laughed and asked why the fight was stopped. They awarded me the Joe Louis Good Sportsmanship because I laughed and did not show disgust and anger that the fight had been stopped. I had not been counted out; it was just stopped. I was not hurt, and the rest of the fight was clearly mine. I still do not understand why it was stopped, and I lost the fight. Dr. Lowman (the

President of Sam Houston University) was called and informed that I had won the sportsmanship award. They sent the award to him, and he awarded it to me at a special ceremony. It was a bittersweet victory in my career.

Jean's eyes slowly followed Roy's gaze to the blurred outline of the rustic training camp, still teaming with curiosity seekers. She thought she read his thoughts.

"I'll be glad," she said," when you have fulfilled the vow to fight that you made so many years ago. It will be wonderful then. No more worry about your getting hurt, no more thoughts of punishing yourself by having to train for days and days and years."

"You know," Roy murmured, "the most important thing in this world, is doing something for others. Henry and Gladys and Tobe have always done that. I have watched them and studied the unselfish way they have served this community. They expect nothing in return and seldom do they get anything. But there is one thing they do get and that's happiness. All of the writers, who have visited them and have written stories about them, have said they were the happiest people they have ever seen.

"Guess I have the happiest brothers and sisters anywhere, Helen, Frances, Wynne, and Patsy—there are no friendlier, finer girls anywhere. And Tobe, Little Henry and Jim Dandy—where on earth are there three more honest, loyal and finer boys? I have so much to be thankful for that I want to spend my life showing other people how those simple little things like love and service can give satisfaction when nothing else can. God intended it to be that way."

Jean had learned the contentment of silence. She sat silently and listened as Roy spoke of things he would later write in his memoirs.

You may have heard me called "the bare foot boxer from Cut and Shoot," and I guess I was as my brother, Tobe, and I fought without shoes for a long time wearing cut-off jeans. My dad, Henry, coached me and worked in my corner wearing overalls. This look was nothing new as Henry wore them every day. We didn't go out deliberately to fool anybody or to look different. The look was authentic. I am surprised that anyone ever thought we did. Even though we were living in a fairly remote area, I was well aware that others had things we did not have. However, I did enjoy the modern conveniences once I got them and really do not want to do without them now.

My greatest love in life was for my family. When I was small, my family was my mother, Gladys, and my father, Henry, and my brothers and sisters. We were very close and were taught to protect each other's backs. They were all a great influence on my life, along with some of my uncles. Uncle Bob and Uncle Jack were two who were memorable among my aunts and uncles on Henry's side. The stories about my dad's father, John Wesley Harris, and his sons, are numerous, and some are almost unbelievable. I come from good, strong, hearty, fighting stock.

On my mother's side was my grandmother, Eunice Murray, who was a very strong advocate for our Lord and Savior, Jesus Christ. She always reminded us where all our blessings came from. My Aunt Dorothy, Aunt Marion, Uncle Harry and Uncle Bob Murray all were very special in our lives. Grandpa Andy Murray worked in the sawmills. He was very fun loving while being a great example for our lives.

I was the second child born to Henry and Gladys Harris, and I was born in the log cabin on the bank of Crystal Creek in the Cut and Shoot area, before the house was moved to the location where the Henry and Gladys Harris family grew up. A new log house was built at this same location, and the little log cabin in which I was born was then used as a barn. The old home where Ma Harris (my dad's mother) lived became vacant after Ma died and was later moved to the Henry Harris log cabin and attached to make a larger home to make room for the eight children they had at the time.

Gladys and Henry's children arrived as follows: Ove Wooten (Tobe) Harris was the first child and was born on March 3, 1932. I was second: Roy Robert Harris, I was born on June 29, 1933. Frank Harris was the next son. He was stillborn, born on October 8, 1935. Helen Gay Harris was my first sister. She was born on June 20, 1937. William Henry Harris followed on November 15, 1939. Frances Wayne Harris was born on November 12, 1941 with Wynne Murray Harris following on September 16, 1943. Patsy Ann Harris, our baby sister, was born on January 22, 1949. James Andrew Harris (Jim Dandy) arrived nine years later on April 23, 1958.

All my brothers and sisters are close to me as well as close to each other. We were taught to fight for and protect the family. Most chose to stay near this area to live. Some wandered off to live other places for a while, but most eventually came back to Cut and Shoot to live. Tobe lives near Conroe. Helen moved to Washington state after working on her PhD. Henry recently moved to Huntsville, Texas with his Cut and Shoot bride, Sandra Groce, sister of my wife, Jean. Frances and Wynne stayed near Cut and Shoot, along with most of their children. My sister, Patsy, married and died young from cancer while living near our old home place. Jim married a local girl, Denise White, and lives in "downtown" Cut and Shoot. I have lived in the Cut and Shoot area my entire life.

Roy further dwells, in part, on his life and family after his marriage to Jean:

God blessed me with a wonderful, loving wife, and allowed us to be together for 53 years before I lost her in 2008. Together, we had eight children, but we lost two at birth. The children have given me nine beautiful grandchildren [as of 2012], with more to come, hopefully. As I mentioned earlier, my family has been the great love, treasure and inspiration for me in my life. Everything I have accomplished has been with them in mind, either my parents and siblings or my wife and children.

For someone as committed to family as Roy, the loss of his first child was a tremendous blow. Here is his description of that most trying time:

Jean and I had decided early that we both wanted a large family, as family was important and close to both of us. I had seven brothers and sisters, at the time, and Jean was from a family of five girls. Our first child was a boy born in Methodist Hospital in Houston. We called him Roy Robin Harris, named for me and for our good friend, Robin Montgomery. Jean had a normal delivery, and the baby appeared to be healthy.

I remember standing at the nursery window watching him and thinking that there were so many babies and only one nurse on duty. I thought it was a normal situation and that everything had been checked out for them and perhaps one nurse was enough. I left with my family to have breakfast and when I returned from eating, the nurse was holding him up by his feet trying to start him breathing. He had developed phlegm and mucus in his mouth, throat and chest and had stopped breathing. Doing everything they could for him, they could not revive him, and he died as I stood outside the window watching. I found out later that the nurse had left for a few minutes to go down the hall and found him choking when she returned. I felt then as I do today that if there had been more help in the nursery, and the problem had been discovered earlier, he would have lived.

Our losing our son brought about several changes at the Methodist Hospital. The hospital began letting husbands go into delivery with their wives. The baby was no longer required to stay in the nursery with the other babies as they were now allowed to stay in the room with the mother upon request. I was all for both changes.

Our going home with empty arms was the hardest thing either of us had ever experienced, and we hoped and prayed it would never happen again. Jean had already had a miscarriage earlier at five months, but this was complete devastation for both of us. We were married five years before we were blessed with a healthy child. We had a problem with phlegm and mucus with each of our other six children at birth, but knew how to look for it and to be prepared.

Our first blessing came in the form of a baby girl on September 27, 1960. We named her Connie Jean Harris. The first thing I remember about her was her head of thick and black curly hair, just like her mother. I was in London fighting Sir Henry Cooper, the European heavyweight champion and was so afraid that I would not make it back in time for the baby's birth. I arrived, however, five days before Jean delivered our beautiful and perfect daughter.

We continued with our blessings having another son, Roy Robert Harris, Jr. on April 27, 1962. Kevin Groce Harris followed on March 13, 1964. Twenty months later on November 29, 1965, Sabrina Kay Harris joined our family. We were not through though, as four years later Ronda Elizabeth Harris was born on August 29, 1973.

We were so proud and delighted with our five children when, with much surprise and delight, we found ourselves expecting six years later, when I was 46 years old and Jean was 44. Resa Lee Harris joined our now perfect family on November 28, 1979. We were experienced parents by then.

Sitting there with Jean in the middle nineteen fifties, dwelling on his life as of a few years before his rendezvous with destiny in the form of a world heavyweight title fight, Roy found contentment in his growing number of friends and fans.

"Everybody has been so nice to me," he observed, "It makes me feel humble. The boys I box are clean and good. I don't remember a single one whom I wouldn't consider my friend. They are just hard working boys trying to do the same thing you and I are trying to do. The only thing I hate about winning is thinking about the sadness that must be in the hearts of those who lose when they are alone with their wives as you and I are now. That's the thing I have tried hard to prepare myself for . . . if I lose. If I ever do, I promise not to worry you by moping all over the place and brooding. That's a big reason I train so hard to win."

Both of them were silent for a long time. A night bird twittered in the tree about them. A reflected red glow from the oil field pulsated like a waving ribbon in the western sky. The flashing golden glows behind them signaled the slow approach of the eternal rains.

"This must never pass away in our lifetime," whispered Roy as though he prayed. "Lou Viscusi has promoted me nearly to the top of the boxing world. I may get to the very tiptop and I may not. Who knows? Henry and Tobe trained me. You have inspired me.

Mr. Viscusi has had faith in me and God has never forsaken me. His will be done . . . but I pray He never takes me away from the creeks."

The Indian sign that accompanied his grandfather's borning was weighing heavily upon one of the world's top-ranked heavyweights. The spoiler of the hopes of many would-be champions felt the fighting Harris blood surging within him. Jeannie squeezed his hand yet again. He breathed a little sigh and relaxed. His mother's blood of the cool methodical Murrays calmed him.

The night was getting chilly. Thunder muttered from the southeast. The young couple lifted themselves from the forest floor and hand in hand followed the lighted pathway to their neat little home.

As they passed through Henry's front yard, Uncle Bob hollered a merry "Hello."

Then Bob continued, "Hey Roy! That little yellow dog you got up in Fort Worth, eight years back. Well, ol' gator just come up out of the pond an gulped him up."

For a moment, the blood of Roy Harris began to churn again. But he quickly accepted the reality of the food chain and the turn of events that claims the life of each creature.

Chapter XII

ROY'S PROFESSIONAL BOXING CAREER

As has been seen, Roy Harris had a glorious amateur career, which prepared him well for the world arena he was about to enter.

I had fought a total of 79 amateur tournament fights over a period of seven years when I decided to begin fighting professionally in 1955. My record was: 70 wins, 3 draws and 6 losses. I probably had several hundred amateur fights at our training camp and at other towns and in high school that are not included in this record. I had four state Golden Gloves championships and was the Southern Division AAU Champion. I also had the coveted Joe Louis sportsmanship award, given to me at the Chicago Golden Gloves in 1955.

My dad, Henry Harris of Cut and Shoot, was one of the South's most successful trainers and coaches and continued to work with me as my trainer. Our home, with its outdoor ring, was considered the amateur fight capital of the state of Texas because of Henry. He could make anyone give his supreme effort while learning. He believed in instilling self-confidence in a person, as he did with me. He worked with me, my brothers, and many other young boys. My whole family was involved in boxing.

Frank A. Godsoe had a column in a Houston newspaper called "Muscle Market " during the 1950s. He reported in one of his columns that "nearly anytime you go by the Harris Hacienda, people will be hitting other people in the mush out in the outdoor ring near the veranda, even at night under the gas flare."

Benny King also came on board and started working with Henry in managing my career. Benny had much knowledge of the game and was considered an authority in the Houston and Texas area. He worked as my manager and was good at getting me fights. Benny had been a pharmacist prior to his getting involved in boxing.

During this early part of my professional career I began to get paid about $75.00 for each fight. We really did not actively campaign for me to fight with better fighters. My mom and dad wanted me to complete my college education at Sam Houston State College in Huntsville, and I still had another year left to go before graduation. I was also in the ROTC program at Sam Houston and was scheduled to go into active duty for two years after graduation. I knew I had some commitments to fulfill before my professional career could be actively addressed. I was determined as they were for me to finish my education and get on with boxing.

In the words of Henry, "We'll take enough fights locally to keep him in good shape, and when he finishes, we'll jump right into the middle of things." This is exactly what we did. My dad knew that I had both the punch and the boxing savvy to succeed at the pro level, and he made me believe it.

My first professional fight was on April 26, 1955 at the Coliseum in Houston. I weighed in at 181 pounds and was in a supporting bout. I fought Tommy Smith, a 175 pounder who was a Korean War veteran from Cincinnati. He was 25 years old and was said to be very impressive in gym drills. We did not have films on him training at that time for me to view, but I was 22 years old, young and cocky and I knew I could take him. I did!

While going through some of my papers, I found a telegram that I received dated April 26, 1955 from a college buddy of mine, Dan Rather. It was sent to a mutual friend of ours, Rex, the Tailor. It reads, "Will you please see that Roy Harris gets my personal best wishes for success tonight. He's an old friend, but I didn't know *where to contact him today. Just tell him that Rather from Sam Houston has confidence in his good right hand." It is signed, Dan Rather. This telegram, along with notes and best wishes from others, encouraged and convinced me that I had made the right decision when I went pro and was now on the right track for professional success.*

So much changed from when I first went pro in 1955 and when I retired from boxing ... During my early pro fights, I wore high top black tennis shoes instead of boxing shoes at the beginning. It was after several pro bouts that I could finally afford a pair of boxing shoes.

As Roy's career began to take off, he thrilled his hometown fans by taking on a fight in Conroe:

During the first professional boxing match ever brought to Conroe, this by the American Legion Post in Montgomery County, I was touted as a "top-notched" card. I fought a tough guy from New Orleans, Ted McDonald, and it was the main event. Tobe Harris and Johnny Hopkins both fought that night also. I won but can't recall if Tobe and Johnny did. What is so memorable about that night was the price of the tickets: It was June 3, 1955. Tickets were priced at $1.60 for adults and 75 cents for children. I know it was a lot of money for 1955 when the average family income was only $4,137; a Ford car cost between $1,606 and

$2,944 and a gallon of gas was 23 cents. As these lines are written in 2011, a popular online ticketing service is selling a ringside seat to Mayweather vs. Marquez for $4,590 each. The exact seat for Pacquiao vs Cotto is currently priced at $10,943. As I mentioned earlier, much has changed in the boxing world.

On November 28, 1955, I had a tough fight. I fought in Tyler against Tyler's pride and joy, a local boxer named Buddy Turman. It was a very important fight in my career, as it was for the Texas Heavyweight Crown. Turman was rated #1 in the state, and I was rated #2 in the heavyweight class. Both of us were young, talented and eager. The ones in the "know" seemed to think that the winner of the fight would be awarded the key to possible "big time" fighting, while the loser would simply return to where he was before the fight.

I was eager for this one. Buddy was a friend, but he was after the title just like I was. I had now had 11 professional fights with 11 wins. Buddy had 11 fights also, but only 10 wins. During the 11th round, Buddy hit my left eye and opened a nasty gash, and I began to bleed profusely. By the end of the last round, I was dripping in blood. I kept my attack active while avoiding his lethal right hand. I did a good job until the 11th round when he cut my eye. I had to push harder as I could feel myself begin to fade. I knew that I had to score big to ensure the judges awarding the rounds to me instead of to the local hero. It was a hard fight, but I took the split decision with no apologies.

Not only did Roy survive that night in Tyler to gain a new title but he also met and became fast friends with perhaps the greatest legend in the history of the sport:

I met a legend that night at the fights that became a good friend of mine. He was Jack Dempsey. Dempsey was an American boxer who held the world heavyweight title from 1919 to 1926. Dempsey's aggressive style and exceptional punching power made him one of the most popular boxers in history. Many of his fights set financial and attendance records, including the first ever million dollar gate. That night he praised me and called me a "brilliant young fighter." We remained friends until his death in 1983, and he actually refereed some of my fights.

I was now making a little money but had none to spare. I worked in the oilfields during the summers when I was not in school plus what I earned boxing. I lived in Cut and Shoot with my wife, Jean, and commuted to Sam Houston State University in Huntsville in an old "clinker", a 1948 Mercury. It was a powerful vehicle even though it was essentially worn out. I also drove this same car to the fights, whether they were in Tyler, Dallas, Houston, etc.

One night I considered myself double lucky! On December 14, 1955 I had a fight in Houston with Ponce de Leon of Ft. Worth. I was lucky to even be there, as I thought I might not make it. My car broke down. A friend of mine, Mickey McCoy, happened to see me in my predicament and stopped to help me. He neglected his own chores to deliver me to Houston from Conroe, which was about 40 miles, to get me to the fight on time. I did make it to the fight on time, and I won a unanimous decision. Dempsey refereed the match.

As Roy's career progressed, he met and defeated several ring greats. One of these was Willie Pastrano. At the time he engaged Roy he was the world's third-ranked heavyweight and formerly the light heavyweight champion of the world.

That fight was a classic. It pitted the rhythmic Pastrano, who played the drums, against the cool methodical Roy Harris. The resulting display of skill and grace was beautiful to behold. Roy won a decision in this bout.

Roy also won a decision over Bob Baker. It was the Baker fight that set him up as the number three contender for Floyd Patterson's crown. Hailing him as the "fastest left in the West," the sports reporters recorded Harris's emergence as the next challenger for boxing's biggest prize.

But before we relate the story of the Patterson fight, it is instructive to review Roy's military career. As will be shown, this career played a pivotal role in the outcome of that fight.

I continued in the ROTC program at Sam Houston until graduation. ROTC, at that time, was a regular class. At times we did physical activities and during other times we learned how the soldiers, the artillery, airplanes and ships worked together in war or combat. After the first two years in ROTC, I did not sign up for the third year. During that summer I got a letter from the government saying, "Congratulations. You have been selected!"

That meant that I was being inducted into the Army. I was still in school, but I had withdrawn from the ROTC and was now eligible for the draft. This would cause me to lose all of the school and all of the ROTC and everything else that I had accomplished in the last three years. I drove to Huntsville with my letter and talked to the Colonel who was head of the ROTC program there in Sam Houston. I asked him if I could continue to go to school and attend ROTC and be released from the draft board letter. He said that he believed he could help me, and he did. I found out later that he was delighted to help me as one more student was needed to sign up for the ROTC to have the quota for the program that year. My grades were high enough to qualify as a candidate for the ROTC program.

While in ROTC, I only had one problem during the entire four years. In my first year, there was an officer in the school ROTC program who evidently did not appreciate the way I shined my shoes for inspection. He disliked my shoe shining so badly that he would say ugly comments to me on the school campus when not in ROTC class.

On the campus one day, I was going to the gymnasium for a Physical Education class. We were walking down the sidewalk toward each other near the school library. This fellow made more ugly remarks about my shoes, and started to hit me, so I thought (He could have been pointing his finger to make a point.) When he moved, I hit him. My fist glanced off his face, so I hit him again, this time harder than I intended. He went down to the sidewalk, his nose bleeding badly, and one side of his face was missing most of the hide from the fall.

The next day I received a letter from the school saying that I was dismissed from Sam Houston and could no longer attend. Another student, named Dan Rather, heard about what happened and got a petition signed by many students to get me reinstated to school. Dr. Lowman was out of town during this incident. When he returned, he called a new board meeting.

Dr. Lowman told the board that he was in charge of the school and he was going to run the school, not the ROTC program. He was there to educate people and not to kick people out where they could not get an education. The board voted unanimously to allow me back in. I returned to school. (I later received a telegram from Dan Rather before and after my fight with Patterson. He was well on his way to being a famous news commentator by then).

When I finished my four years in the ROTC program and graduated from Sam Houston in 1956, I had to attend some active duty before I would receive a 2nd Lieutenant commission. I had some time before active duty, so I got a job teaching school in Cut and Shoot to continue to make weekly meetings with the military in Huntsville. I was in the Army Reserves. We almost activated when the Cuban Missile Crisis occurred, but evidently President Kennedy stood up enough to cause the Russians to back down and remove their missiles from Cuba.

Sometime during the following year I received a letter from the military that my two years active duty had been changed to six months because the Reserve Military was running low on money. I continued teaching in Cut and Shoot for two years before I was called to active duty.

I went to Ft. Sill, Oklahoma and was placed in an artillery school and spent my entire six months stationed there. I was given a promotion to 1st Lieutenant. I was still obligated in the military as a reserve officer for a total of twelve years, including my active duty. During the last part of my twelve years I was promoted to Captain.

Roy was stationed at Ft. Sill from January until July of 1958. It is here that the story impacts the course of his fight with Floyd Patterson. He came back to Cut and Shoot for about a week or two before going to California. He needed to be in California as soon as possible, for publicity and training for the big fight that was scheduled for August 18th.

My dad and I loaded up and headed for Los Angeles, California. Jean was discouraged from joining me at that time by my manager, Lou Viscusi, and my trainer, Bill Gore. I disagreed with them, but they were the bosses. She stayed in Cut and Shoot and continued working and joined me just before the fight.

We stayed in the mountains near Los Angeles in a motel where I began my training. I did roadwork in the mornings and sparred along with punching the bag in the evenings. I ate a high protein diet not knowing that it would cause me to lose weight. I had always believed that I was supposed to cut out all starches and sugar, but I was totally ignorant about nutrition and what I should do or should not do. No one helped me with nutrition during my training as following a good nutritious diet was not popular or the thing to do at that time.

Lou Viscusi and Bill Gore remained in Houston during this time with Joe Brown, the World's Lightweight Champion, who was training for a title bout. Denny McMahon, who was a friend of Lou Viscusi, stayed with me in California. He was a good man, but we did not have much communication between us. He did not really know me, or what I needed.

It is here that we see the pivotal importance of Roy's commitment to the military, the obstacle that it presented to adequate preparation for the big fight:

During my six-month active duty in the Army, I was not allowed to spar with any other soldier. Enlisted people were not allowed to box with officers, so I was unable to get any sparring for about six months during the time leading up to my title bout. This definitely put me at a disadvantage. All I could do to train was to run and punch the bag.

While I was in California and Lou came to work with me after Joe Brown's fight in Houston and saw me running, he said he was going to cancel the fight. I asked why, and he replied that I was not ready or able to fight. He said that something was wrong with me. I agreed that something was wrong, but I did not know what it was or what to do about it.

Lou wanted to postpone the fight, but I disagreed. I wanted to fight. He told me that I needed to start getting in shape and said that he thought that I was low in carbohydrates. He wanted me to drink two bottles of beer each evening to build my weight back up. As I do not drink, I told that I was not going to drink any beer and questioned whose side he was on. He told me that we did not have much time left, and I needed to start building up the carbs immediately. I did not drink any beer for about a week— that was only a week before the fight.

After continually losing about two pounds a day and getting weaker each day, I told him to bring on the beer, and I would drink it. I had wasted a week, which I needed badly. If only I had known enough about nutrition, I could have solved my problem without drinking beer, which put weight on but did not necessarily build energy. But I knew nothing about it. If I had listened to Lou when he first got there I might have regained my energy and won the fight. But, for some reason, it did not happen that way. I gained some of my weight back, but not my energy. I weighed in at 187, which should have been around 195 pounds. Between not training as I should have been during my six months in service, not eating a proper nutritious diet, not listening to Lou and missing Jean, I did not *win. The two weeks before the fight were the most miserable two weeks of my life.*

In addition to the problems outlined here by Roy, geography also played a negative role. Training on a mountain, then fighting below in Los Angeles was a strain on the lungs. At any rate, as Roy said, the fight went twelve rounds which is normal now for a championship fight.

Back home, on that warm summer night most of the Cut and Shoot clansmen, along with scores of local fans, gathered at Conroe's drive-in theater to view the fight on a special closed circuit hook-up. It was a most colorful evening with guitars twanging and people dancing and clapping their hands. Everyone felt that Roy would soon be champion. Nor did the feeling subside until very late in the fight.

During an early round Roy sent Patterson to the floor and the crowd in the theater went wild. Horns blew, people shouted and soft drinks and corn squeezing's sallied forth to wet the wings of birds flying overhead because they had been scared from their roosts by the noise. But Patterson struggled to his feet. Still Roy pressed him, pounding with his left, rights and counters to the body and to the head.

This, though, was the night that Patterson was to prove himself to the world as a worthy champion. He not only survived the knockdown, but he came on strong as the fight progressed to gradually penetrate more and more Roy's defenses as, in his weakened condition, Roy faded in the latter rounds. Around the eighth round, Roy had begun to bleed profusely and to exhibit protruding bruises to the head and body.

Still Roy fought gamely on. The Cut and Shoot veteran of thousands of yard fights with his brother, Tobe, knew that this was his only chance to prove himself to his rough but lovable kinsmen. Mustering all the courage nurtured through wrestling alligators and other denizens of the swamplands, Roy fought on.

The continuous roar of the huge crowd brought to Roy memories of wilderness noises just after dark when the wild things begin to roam. Never, however, had he encountered anything like the wild equivalent of a Floyd Patterson intent on redeeming himself for being floored for the first time. Although Patterson definitely took charge of the fight in the latter rounds, Roy still stubbornly maintained his ground, refusing to surrender. However, destiny lay that night with the champion, not the challenger. After twelve bruising rounds of a scheduled fifteen round fight, the referee raised Patterson's hand in victory on a T.K.O. technicality.

After the fight, Roy had nothing but praise for Patterson. His only statement in his defense was, "I did my best." It was only long after the event that Roy finally agreed to respond to persistent questioners and list some of the trials, outlined here, that he went through en route to the grand encounter in Los Angeles.

In defeat, Roy gained a tremendous moral victory. He had fulfilled his vow of long ago to earn the respect of the Robin Hood of the boomer days and his rugged clansmen by becoming one of the strongest of the realm. Now he could relax and pursue his true peaceful nature.

And great has been the success thereof.

Chapter XIII

THE AFTERMATH

Seldom if ever has a fighter lost a world-class fight, such as did Roy Harris, and re-bounded to such adoration and success in multiple endeavors. It is difficult to imagine Roy's life after the Patterson Fight being any better served, had he been victorious that August night in 1958. A brief survey here will reflect how, with the same verve, courage, and intelligence portrayed in his boxing career, he embraced a life charged meaningfully with accomplishment and service to humanity.

World interest and enthusiasm for the "Battler from the Backwoods" was at such a high level during the build up for the fight that the U.S. postal service felt constrained to establish in Cut and Shoot a post office. Though the community had long since received its name, it was only on August 18, 1958, the exact date of the fight, that it received a post office. According to Amy Wade, the town's secretary, the timing was arranged to coincide with the Harris-Patterson Fight. The reason was the overwhelming mail from across the globe addressed to "Roy Harris, Cut and Shoot, Texas".

In 1958, I fought Floyd Patterson for the World Heavyweight title in boxing and began receiving a lot of fan mail. So much mail was addressed to "Roy Harris, Cut and Shoot, Texas" that the U.S. Postal Service granted a franchise post office to the town. Mr. T.J. Rutledge lived in the area, having moved here from Houston with his family. He received the appointment as the first Post Master of Cut and Shoot.

Having thus established a base for further expansion, the citizens surrounding the area of the post office began to seek incorporation as a bona fide community.

Roy tells how Mr. Rutledge took a lead in that quest:

He began to tell me that I needed to incorporate Cut and Shoot and make it a legal city before Houston and Conroe could annex us. We began to talk with other leading citizens of Cut and Shoot to see if they agreed that we should be incorporated. Mr. Rutledge started a campaign to get signatures of people who were in favor of incorporation. He was the Post Master and most of the people came by daily to get their mail, and he would get them to sign the petition for an election to incorporate Cut and Shoot.

In the following piece Roy refers to himself as the county clerk and as an attorney, occurrences we will address more fully in due course in this chapter:

I was the County Clerk of Montgomery County during this time as well as an attorney. I had the county surveyor, Jake Neeves, prepare a survey of the proposed city of Cut and Shoot. Mr. Neeves did the survey without charging Cut and Shoot a fee for his work. Mr. Rutledge acquired enough names on the petition to have an election, which was held by the Commissioner's Court approving the election. Cut and Shoot was established as a city in Texas in 1969. A later election elected all of the officials to run the new city. Glen (Skinny) Gilbert and E. L. (Babe) Musgrove paid for the cost of the election.

Thelbert Sheffield was the first town Marshall.

During the naming of Cut and Shoot, there were probably no more than 25 families in the area. It had grown to a population of 1700 by 2011. Cut and Shoot has had a reputation all my life as being remote and wild where anything was legal if you did not get caught.

As Roy returned home from his championship bout to a hero's welcome, he settled in to find the direction for the remainder of his life. His fertile brain sensing that the area was on the verge of a tremendous upsurge in growth, he rightly surmised that the real estate business was rife with opportunity.

In his memoirs, Roy states that initially, however, for a short while, he ventured back to school teaching:

It was not long that I realized that teachers did not make a lot of money, and I wanted a good life for my family, like my father had. I began looking around for something I could do to earn a better living as my first year's pay as a teacher was only $2,800 for the entire year.

Real estate seemed interesting to me. I became a real estate broker by taking the state test and began my life long business. I went to work for Barney Wiggins in Livingston. Jean and I loaded up our family and moved there. We kept our home in Cut and Shoot, however, to where we soon returned.

I received my Broker's License in 1962 and began listing property in the state of Texas. I also bought land in Arkansas. I have often been accused of being too lazy to hold a full time job, and that is the reason I sold real estate. I could set my own hours (That really isn't all true.)

I enjoyed finding a piece of property and matching it with a person who wanted and liked it. I majored in Vocational Agriculture at Sam Houston and felt that I knew a lot about the land and how to use it for agricultural purposes. I was raised on a poor sandy land farm and was used to producing the kind of crops that were most adaptable to our area. I was qualified to be what is called in Montgomery County the County Agent. I could tell folks what land was good for and how they could use it. I could tell them how to harvest the timber for the best results. I enjoyed talking to people and felt that folks could trust me, as I knew what I was talking about.

Most people think I earned my money from boxing. I did not. Boxing opened doors for me. Boxing gave me the ability to be well known, and it helped me to prosper in real estate and politics.

And what a political career Roy did have, amazing! But let him tell the story:

While I was working in Livingston, I was politicking for Judge Ernest Coker, who was running for reelection for District Judge. He told me that the present County Clerk of Montgomery County, Bud Hooper, was not going to run for reelection and that I should register, myself. He said that it was a good job, and I would get to meet a lot of people in the Clerk's office, and because I was so well known from boxing and was a local candidate, I would have a good chance to win the election.

When I decided to run for County Clerk, Republicans were not in favor in Montgomery County. I ran as a Democrat as did most of the other politicians at that time. During the following years while I was in office, the Republicans began to gain popularity, and most politicians shifted their party affiliation from the Democrats to the Republican Party.

Today, with so many citizens voting a straight Republican ticket, I would have lost the election, as I never changed my affiliation. I continued to feel an obligation to the Democrats, who held all of the offices in Montgomery County when I originally ran for County Clerk. My loyalties stayed with the Democratic Party, although I realized that I no longer believed as they did. My last two years in office, I was the lone democrat [holding a county office].

I ran and won the election and became County Clerk in January of 1967. I continued as County Clerk of Montgomery County for 28 years, or seven 4-year terms.

We kept records of all of the Commissioner's Court meetings, all of the Civil County Court cases, and all other misdemeanor records. Anytime a record was found and no one knew what to do with it, it would be given to the County Clerk for safekeeping. Sometimes I felt that my office was a catchall! We kept all deed records and real property or land records. The only *records we did not keep were District Court Records and felony records. The District Court also kept the Civil Records that were about cases of $5,000 or more.*

My office handled all election records. I appointed people to become the Election Precinct Chairman, if one were not already available, for each of the different precincts. The Commissioner's Court approved my choices. If anyone wanted to run for a particular Precinct Chairman, he or she could be put on a ballot and run for the office.

The Chairman would then run the election in his or her precinct. The sheriff's office would deliver all of the materials and booths that were needed for the elections to the Precinct Chairman where the election would be held. After the election, the Chairman would deliver back to my office, all unused materials and all ballots with the results from that precinct. My staff would complete the results and announce the winners. This was all done under the jurisdiction of the Commissioner's Court.

Interesting is how Roy, in order to increase his proficiency as County Clerk, decided to add yet another layer to his accomplishments, that of becoming an attorney. It shows that the old competitive fires were ever burning:

While I was in the Clerk's office, I worked with many lawyers. I listened to them talk about happenings in and out of the courtroom. I enjoyed listening to them and would offer an opinion or add something to what had just been said. Some of the lawyers welcomed my opinions, while others did not, telling me that I was not a lawyer and did not know what I was talking about. I decided that I wanted to be a lawyer myself.

As I had to work full time and could not go to law school, I had to find another way. I discovered that I could become a lawyer without going to law school as long as I passed the State Bar. I found out that I could qualify to take the state bar by studying in a law office for a certain period of time. I began to work in the offices of Hopkins and Alworth, local Conroe attorneys. I worked evenings and weekends to get my hours in.

I hired a tutor to help me. He was a law student in Houston. He would work with me after my work in the evenings and any other time we could find to study. When I took the bar, I passed all the sections of the test except one. I made a D, which was not acceptable. About six months later, I had to retake the whole test. On September 26, 1972, I passed the entire test and became a County Lawyer. (My tutor also passed)

My studying law and becoming an attorney enabled me to better understand the complexities of the courts and to better serve the people as County Clerk of Montgomery County.

Roy Harris's metamorphosis from rustic backwoodsman to heavyweight contender to successful lawyer, businessman and politician mirrors that of the new Cut and Shoot. The robust spirit of the original clansmen has permeated the region, causing it to gain a place alongside the most literate and progressive areas of the nation.

All members of the Harris clan have been very successful. Among them are attorneys, medical doctors and of course real estate moguls. And Roy's younger brother, Henry, wealthy in his own right via real estate, remains, in the Harris tradition, a trainer of boxers. As of this writing, he is sponsoring a very likely prospect for a world championship, Alfonzo "El Tigre" Lopez.

At clan gatherings, descendants of the original rough riders and their friends tell tales of the old days, while relishing the common bond to which such history connects them.

Some of their favorite tales are of the late Coon Massey. We will relate a tale of one of Roy's most memorable meetings on the trail with the latter day Coon. Roy gives evidence of Coon's prowess in business, knowing how to capitalize on emerging trends:

Coon became well known as the "hog boy of Cut and Shoot." He, as well as other people in the area such as Henry, raised hogs, which ran loose and free in the woods. It was known as "open range" for all animals and livestock. Each person with livestock in the area had to register a mark that they owned in the County Clerk's office in the county. They also had to register a brand for horses and cattle if theirs ran loose on the open range. The farmers, during the open range, had to fence around their garden and farm products to keep livestock and wild game from destroying their food crops. The open range (in Cut and Shoot) came to an end in the 1950s. People who owned cattle, horses, hogs, goats, sheep and other livestock had to identify and gather their livestock from others in the open range and place them in a livestock proof fence. He was responsible for keeping them off roads and out of other people's gardens and properties.

Coon saw this condition as an opportunity to buy and sell cattle, hogs and other livestock. The hogs became the most productive business for him, as he could carry them in the back of his truck. Many people could not afford to gather up their livestock from the open range. Coon would buy all of the hogs in the owner's marks; he then would have to go into the woods with his dogs and capture the hogs and fatten them with corn and grain. He would butcher the hogs or sell them on foot to any buyer who wanted a hog. He began to tell people that Roy Rogers was the King *of the Cowboys and Coon Massey was the King of the Hog-boys! He became well known in the Cut and Shoot area because he sold many hogs to many different people around the area.*

We will now relate the story of Roy meeting the latter day Coon, the king of the hog-boys, on the trail.

Coon greeted him, "Hey ole Buddy, you yet shot aire deer?"

Roy replied, "No, Coon, have you?"

"I haven't yet got aire shell to shoot him with," replied Coon who was limping along and holding his behind with one hand and his rifle with the other, all the while looking forlornly at his little spaniel dog with a big red nose.

"See that ole gentleman there, he be World Champion Squirrel dog," bragged Coon. "This mornin' you know what that gentleman treed?"

Roy admitted that he didn't, so Coon told him. "That gentleman treed a honey bee." Roy saw that that was obvious from the swelling on the champion's nose.

"But," Roy asked, "tell me, ol' partner, why are you limping?

"Well, it's like this," Coon replied, "it's a tale about my tail, and a real legend of an experience."

One of Coon's sons sent him a gun from Alaska, where the boy lived and worked for an oil company. He asked Coon to sell it for him and send him the money. Coon decided to sell the gun (double barrel shot gun) to Lamar Lambert who was looking for a gun to buy. They took the gun out one night to test it by shooting rabbits; they had killed one and decided to go to another location in the oil field to look for more rabbits. The gun, however, had a flaw that Coon did not know about. When jarred, it would sometimes fire both barrels without any trigger action. Coon had reloaded the gun and laid it in the back seat of the car. He decided to sit in the back seat and crawled in and sat down. Both barrels went off, blowing the cheeks of Coon's tail end off!

Lamar got him out of the car and took him to the front where the lights of the car allowed him to see how much damage had been done. Lamar was afraid that Coon would not live to get to the hospital; he got Coon back in the car and drove away at a rapid rate of speed. The car was going so fast that Coon became scared and told Lamar to slow the buggy down or they may never get to the hospital!

Finally they arrived at the hospital, but there were no doctors on duty at the time. The nurses called the doctor to come quickly. Coon was sat on a gurney; as he sat there, blood ran from his butt onto the floor and down the hall for about twenty-five or thirty feet where it puddled up. After the doctor arrived, he asked Coon how he felt. Coon replied, "I have felt worse when I stumped my old sore toe, and I have felt better while eating chicken." The doctor trimmed the remaining cheeks off Coon's tail end.

Coon's wife, Annie Mae, was a very devout Christian. She had long tried to get Coon to go to church with her and believed this would be an ideal time (due to his close brush with death) for the preacher to talk to and pray with Coon and to get him to get his foot in the pathway of righteousness. Coon was afraid to talk with the preacher for fear of how Henry Harris would tell the story. They always loved to joke around with each other and, in anticipation of what Henry might say Coon did not want the preacher to hear his great friend's version of the story!

The preacher asked Coon if he had thought about God when the accident happened; Coon said, "I believe that I did mention His name in a vile sort of way." The preacher asked him, "How is that, Mr. Massey?" Coon replied, "I said God o' Mighty, I believe that I have blowed my tail plum off!" The preacher promptly left. Later, while talking with others about his accident,

Coon was heard to say that he really did not mind losing his tail end except he missed that cushion he was used to sitting on.

As Roy and Coon met on the trail and Coon related the story of the great shooting, both Roy and Coon, himself, sat on a hackberry stump and laughed at the tale of Coon's tragedies. And the two millionaires talked about Coon's lack of shotgun shells "to shoot 'aire deer with" with the same unassuming air that "Old Hickory", Andrew Jackson, used when he assumed the Presidency of the United States. They walked tall and ferociously proud, humble but un-intimidated, with only God and common sense to guide them. Not only they, but also all the clansmen of Cut and Shoot who once roamed the San Jacinto River bottomlands had walked that way.

"Ah, Cut and Shoot!" sighed Roy, "What a name in a tangled land along a Saintly River." He was at peace as he talked with Coon and watched the lightning flashing from the clouds forever belching out of the Mexican Sea. Like the lightning, the words of David, the Psalmist, flashed across his mind: "I will extol thee, O Lord," whispered Roy spontaneously. "For thou hast lifted me up and hast not made my foes to rejoice over me."

Reverently, Coon whispered, "Amen".

Addendum:

ROY ROBERT HARRIS, SR.

The following is a summary of Roy's life and achievements, extracted from notes in his memoirs:

Son of Gladys Murray and Henry Harris, Sr. Roy Harris was born June 29, 1933, one of eight children. Roy attended Conroe Schools and graduated from Conroe High School in 1951. He started boxing at the tender age of five as a "live in" sparring partner of his older brother, Tobe, who loved to box. Their father, Henry, who had boxed several top contenders and was undefeated, coached them.

He received a certificate (at 12 years of age) from Travis Junior High School in Conroe for Boxing. His coaches were the popular principal, J.T. Montgomery, and Glen Buffaloe, who was the All Service Champion and a sparring partner for Joe Louis during World War II.

Won Regional Golden Gloves six years in a row, starting in 1950. Won State Golden Gloves four years in a row: 1952, 1953, 1954 and 1955. He received silver and ruby championship rings for each of these years.

Won the State Olympic Trials in Houston in 1952 but did not get to go to Nationals. Floyd Patterson won the Olympics that year.

Won the Joe Louis Sportsmanship Award at the National Golden Gloves in Chicago, 1955.

Was in ROTC at Sam Houston State and reached the rank of 2nd Lieutenant in Artillery Army Reserve in 1957; went into active duty shortly afterwards in the Army and left the Army as a Captain.

Graduated from Sam Houston State in 1956 with a Bachelor of Science Degree. He taught school in Willis High School, Stephen F. Austin Elementary in Cut and Shoot and William B. Travis Jr. High School in Conroe from 1955-1957.

Post Office opened in Cut and Shoot in 1958 to handle all of the fan mail he was receiving. Fans would (and still do) mail letters addressed to Roy Harris, Cut and Shoot, Texas, USA.

Turned Pro on April 26, 1955.

Received the Progress Award from Ring Magazine for the Greatest Advancement in Boxing in 1957.

As a professional, won the Texas State Heavyweight Championship from Buddy Turman in 1955; Won the Heavyweight Championship of the South from Oscar Pharo in 1956; Rated one of the top three fighters in the world in 1958; Before the Patterson Heavyweight Title fight his record was 22 fights and 22 wins—nine by KO.

Fought Floyd Patterson for the World Heavyweight title on August 18th, 1958 in Wrigley Field, Los Angeles, California.

Beginning in 1959, the Houston Golden Glove Tournament awarded a Roy Harris Trophy to the most courageous boxer in the tournament.

Roy was featured in several articles (with photos) in Time Magazine, Saturday Evening Post, True Boxing Yearbook Magazine and Life Magazine. He was on the cover of Sports Illustrated two times and on the cover of Ring Magazine three times. He was included in the World Book Encyclopedia along with Wikipedia Online. He has several videos from You Tube.

He recorded a song, "Cut and Shoot, Texas, USA" for Decca Records in 1958.[On the flip side of that record was a song written by Robin Montgomery, "Desert in the Sky"]

In 1959,he received the Sports Writers Honor, "The Southwesterner of the Year", the first pro athlete to receive the coveted award.

He passed the Texas State Real Estate test and became a broker in 1960. He served as the County Clerk of Montgomery County from 1967 to 1995 for a total of 28 years. In 1972, he passed the State Bar and became an Attorney at Law.

Roy sponsored the little league team called the "Roy Harris Wildcats" for 12 to 13 years, a team which his brother, Henry Harris, coached. Twice the team advanced to the State Championship. Many leaders of our community played on this team. Two are well known local coaches. One of these, Danny Freeman, coached Willis baseball for 24 years and became a coach at Conroe High School. The other, Toby York, played on the Wildcats and went on to become a coach and then Superintendent of Schools.

The book, "Cut'n Shoot Texas: Roy Harris-Battler from the Backwoods," was written by Robin Montgomery and published in 1984 [Eakin Press].

Roy married Gloria Jean Groce on September 24, 1955 and the couple had six children: Connie Jean Harris, Roy Robert Harris, Jr., Kevin Groce Harris, Sabrina Kay Harris, Ronda Elizabeth Harris and Resa Lee Harris. He has nine grandchildren [as of 2011]: Blake Nelson, Cassie Nelson, Victoria Nelson, Lynnsey Harris, Skylar Harris, Devin Harris, Ethan Harris, Blane Harris and Makayla Harris.

As a crowning example of the acclaim in which his neighbors continued to hold him, as the first decade of the 21st century wound down, the Conroe City Council declared August 18th, the date on which he fought for the world's heavyweight title in 1958, as "Roy Harris Day."

About the Authors

Robin Navarro Montgomery: (co-author with Roy Harris, see below)

Degrees:

PhD, political science, University of Oklahoma
MA, Latin American Studies, University of Oklahoma
MA, Education-English, Sam Houston St. University
B.A. History, University of Texas, Austin
B.S. Biology-Chemistry, Sam Houston St. University

Career:

Professor, Oklahoma, European Theater, Oxford Graduate School
Currently, president of Texas Center for Regional Studies

Publications:

Nine books
Dozens of articles, national security journals and history, and scholarly paper presentations
Newspaper columnist, both on current events and local history

Family:

married, four children

regional interest

Have held numerous offices, such as presidencies of local history, political organizations orchestrated several public events, including a coming event this April, 200th anniversary 1st Republic of Texas, Athlete in high school, quarterback, et al--leader of a musical group

_____

Roy Harris, co-author

The book is about him, world class boxer, attorney, successful politician, and businessman.